Snow Over The Pines

Property of
Elaine Attias

WORKS BY REWI ALLEY

POEMS

Gung Ho!: *Christchurch 1948*
Leaves from a Sandan Notebook: *Christchurch 1950*
Fragments from Living Peking: *Christchurch 1955*
This is China Today: *Christchurch 1957*
Beyond the Withered Oak: *Christchurch 1962*
Who is the Enemy?: *Peking 1964*
The Mistake: *Christchurch 1965*
What is Sin?: *Christchurch 1967*
Poems of Protest: *Christchurch 1970*
Upsurge: *Christchurch 1970*
73—Man to Be: *Christchurch 1971*
Winds of Change: *Christchurch 1972*
Poems for Aotea-roa: *Auckland 1972*
Walkabout: *Melbourne, Australia 1973*
Over China's Hills of Blue: *Christchurch 1974*
Today and Tomorrow: *Christchurch 1975*
Snow over the Pines: *Christchurch 1977*

TRANSLATIONS OF CHINESE POETRY

Peace Through the Ages: *Peking 1954*
The People Speak Out: *Peking 1954*
Lament of a Soldier's Wife: *Hanoi*
The People Sing: *Peking 1958*
Poems of Revolt: *Peking 1962*
Tu Fu: Selected Poems: *Peking 1962*
Not a Dog: *Peking 1962*
The Eighteen Laments: *Peking 1963*

PROSE

Yo Banfa!: *Shanghai 1952, Peking 1955, Auckland 1976*
Peking Opera: *Peking 1953*
The People Have Strength: *Peking 1954*
Spring in Vietnam: *Christchurch 1956*
Land of the Morning Calm: Christchurch *1956*
Buffalo Boys of Vietnam: *Hanoi 1956*
Children of the Dawn: *Peking 1956*
Journey to Outer Mongolia: *Christchurch 1957*
Human China: *Christchurch 1957*
Stories Out of China: *Peking 1958*
Sandan: An Adventure in Creative Education: *Christchurch 1959*
Towards a People's Japan: *Christchurch 1960*
Three Conferences: *Christchurch 1961*
China's Hinterland: *Peking 1961*
Land and Folk in Kiangsi: *Peking 1962*
Among the Hills and Streams of Hunan: *Peking 1963*
Our Seven—Their Five: *Peking 1963*
In the Spirit of Hunghu: *Peking 1966*
Fruition: *Christchurch 1967*
Oceania: *Christchurch 1971*
Some Chinese Children: *Christchurch 1972*
The Prisoners: *Christchurch 1972*
Children 1962-1972: *Peking 1973* (Photographs)
A Highway and an Old Chinese Doctor: *Christchurch 1973*
The Rebels: *Auckland 1973*
Travels in China: *Peking 1973*
Taiwan: *Auckland 1973, 1976*
Vaster Landets Imperialism I Kana: *Stockholm 1974* with Hans
    Miller (in Swedish)
La Chine—Une Autre Qualitié du Vie. In collaboration with W.
    Burchett (in French)
China—The Quality of Life: Wilfred Burchett with Rewi Alley:
    Penguin Books 1976

Snow Over The Pines

Poems by *REWI ALLEY*

———

With a Foreword by
George Hatem (Ma Hai-teh) M.D.

———

The New Zealand-China Friendship Society
and
The Progressive Book Society
1977

Publishers' addresses:

The New Zealand-China Friendship Society (Inc.)
P.O. Box 3460, Auckland, New Zealand.

The Progressive Book Society, Ltd.,
P.O. Box 5151, Auckland, New Zealand.

PRINTED AT THE CAXTON PRESS
CHRISTCHURCH NEW ZEALAND

CONTENTS

PART II. *From Hainan to Heilungkiang*

FOREWORD

IT is not given to many men to live in two worlds and know deeply the aspirations and hopes and struggles that make up those worlds — China and New Zealand. Rewi Alley, a very dear comrade, friend and mentor, is both a New Zealander and a Chinese, has lived, loved, struggled and worked for and with the Chinese people for a full half century. He has travelled over the length and breadth of the land of the "black-haired people". He has worked on the northern and western borders including the Khinghan Ranges with coverings of "Snow and Pines" as well as in the southern tropical island of Hainan. He has lived in the hot humid plains of the coast of China and in the high plateaus of the Kunlun. By foot and by cart, by any means available over the years, Rewi moves and works among the people, savouring their triumphs after the Liberation. And he has participated in the struggle over the years. The sufferings, the struggles and the joys of the Chinese people have been the sufferings, struggles and joys of Rewi Alley, as a participant and not as an observer.

With keen political insight developed over a span of eighty years, (Rewi is eighty this year) and with a lasting deep love for his chosen people he rejoices over the present upsurge in China following the removal of the "Gang of Four", Wang Hung-wen, Chang Chun-chiao, Chiang Ching and Yao Wen-yuan. In his works and writings he delineates the tremendous release of human energy now going on in China, guided by another wise leadership in the Central Committee of the Chinese Communist Party. Chairman Hua Kuo-feng with the support of the people and the old stalwart revolutionaries of the Long March and the new generation of comrades that emerged after that epic, move forward together in unity to make up for the grievous loss of the triumvirate of the Chinese Revolution — Mao Tse-tung, Chou En-lai and Chu Teh and the tragic losses the Chinese people suffered from the great earthquakes and floods in 1976.

We are privileged to share some of Rewi Alley's thoughts and feelings distilled from such a rich historical experience. In his latest work, *Snow Over The Pines*, there are many rich

9

treasures, a generous collection of gems strung on the kaleidoscope of history. He invites us to witness the unrolling of events and partake in the magnificent changes going on as they appear in his eyes and his broad vision. Rewi Alley has crystalised his experience and knowledge of this great land and its people in his writings, of which the present work is an example. He writes from a heart molded with a calm and cool approach but not as a neutral, as a man deeply committed and concerned. He not only explains the world of China that he works in but together with 800 million of his comrades-in-arms tries to change it.

In the poetic cadences and rhythms of *Snow Over The Pines* we feel the vibration of millions of hearts and hands moving forward, making progress through struggle. We see glimpses of determination by the Chinese people to level to the ground the shibboleths of the Confucian ways; we see an iron will of a unified people determined to remove both man-made and nature-made obstructions. With a shake of 800 million shoulders dams, dykes and dynamos spring up, structures of the mind and matter are built in the spirit of learning from Tachai in agriculture and from Taching in industry and this is coupled with intense efforts in science, culture, education and health to provide support. The emerging new social patterns in China foretell the socialist flowering of a new man and a new land. A man reaching for the stars.

Rewi Alley over the span of many a year has written many books of prose and poetry. *Snow Over The Pines* is the latest in a series published by his myriad of admiring friends in New Zealand. As with his other writings, he contributes of himself giving a dedication to bring us understanding and friendship, broadening our vision and deepening our knowledge of the good people of China who are making their old land into a youthful land with hundreds of millions of the young growing up and learning through struggle, at the side of their elders, why they are living and where they are going.

Snow Over The Pines is part and parcel of Rewi's and China's world.

GEORGE HATEM (MA HAI-TEH)

Peking, June, 1977

10

PREFACE

"You can't sell poetry! Why bother with it?"

So do I look back over verse already written, old n.
mingling with things seen through the days since the last cor.
tion was published, and decide that, after all, it would be best
to put down at least some of the impressions gained before they
fade out. Who knows? They may strike a chord somewhere, and
help a little to understanding.

Priorities change, but the story of this quarter of the people
of the world in their struggle against poverty and the old order
which held them down so bitterly, is a human epic that never
tires one to sing about.

Each new success, whether along the base of the Kunlun
mountains fronting the great desert, or amongst the peaks of Da
Liang Shan where the Yi people now build anew, or around
long-settled areas where so much has yet to be conquered, gives
its thrill. People fighting together to make bad lands into good
lands, and so improve the quality of their lives as they reach out
in comradeship with other working people like themselves. The
sight of the Chinese people building a segment of our globe not
dedicated to national chauvinism, but to the basic idea of changing the thinking of mankind from "grab" to "give", by their
example, is an inspiring one. Peoples of the world have much
to learn from China's experience.

The impressions of a lone New Zealander, travelling for more
than fifty years over the highways and by-ways of this land, may
be of some use, then, to the many in the west who want to learn
more about this part of the world; learn, because only too
obviously the old everyone-for-himself system they live under no
longer works, and everywhere peoples stir, knowing that something is wrong, and ways must be found to put wrongs right.
Russia ever tries to keep subject peoples from murmuring, and
to extend its lands, looking hungrily on China's North Eastern
provinces, old lusts re-activated. The spirit of "What you have
I want", the core of imperialism, is still the dominant thinking
amongst too many. China gallantly sets out to build a basis for
a better way, maintaining the spirit of the people, despite all.

11

Shirley Barton, with the help of friends in New Zealand, has worked hard on re-typing, editing and publishing this manuscript. My brother, Pip, has done his best to help as usual. People come to Peking from many lands, and amongst them an old American friend, Manny Granich, and Berte his wife, who have helped so much to make this present volume possible. Old comrades, Drs Hans Miller and Ma Hai-teh, have read most of the poems and have helped with constructive criticism. All of these I thank.

REWI ALLEY,
Peking, Summer, 1977.

PART I

Written in Peking and Peitaiho

Dr George Hatem   Rewi Alley   Dr Hans Miller
(Dr Ma Hei-teh)

SNOW OVER THE PINES

What crop grows
without weeds trying to smother
the young grain shoots;
what harvest is gained without
insect pests having to be dealt
with, or else typhoon, drought,
flood or earthquake? Enemies
infiltrate, as is the nature of things.
Well did the Chinese fighter, Chen Yi, write,
"Snow over the pines
which grow so free and straight;
if you would see how grand
they are, just wait for the snow
to melt."
Life is a thing
of struggle; be not surprised
when rank weeds pretending
to be grain, are plucked ruthlessly
from amongst the real.

In China, too, the drive to solve
basic problems has to go hand in hand
with cleansing the ranks; the gang
of four planted its supporters cunningly
enough, but today the people see through
the mist of verbiage that obscured,
demand progress on every front.
"We made revolution in order to succeed!
Now let there be more success!" they cry.

Peking, 11 February, 1977

AUTOBIOGRAPHY

The last entry to this story
evades me; perhaps it was typed,
maybe not; the incidents in it
already vanishing into the mist
of half-forgotten memories; so that
now a new start is made, beginning
in 1973, when after two weeks
seeing folk in New Zealand, the
road led through six Australian states
where around the fringes one could
at least get a breath of the challenge
that faces young Australia today;
meeting many folk devoted to the idea
of making friendship with China,
their now so near neighbour. Back
in Peking and with summer coming, off
to the Apa Tibetan region that lies
on the trail of the Long March, seeing
something of the new Tibetan, what
he has done to his grasslands, and to his
own society. It was good to
look at the new Ma Er Ken, and the bright
school at Chokerchi, visit the Chiang
folk in Wenchuan, and then to fly on
to the familiar Northwest again; oil wells
at Yumen, the merciless old
Gobi being rolled back, belts of forest,
thousands of wells bringing up waters
that have flowed under folk dying for the
want of water down through the ages;
going to see the Tienchu Tibetans, and
the new sheep, the new people who
herd them. And the one more summer
at Peitaiho, which included a trip
around the hinterland with George*

---

*Dr George Hatem (Dr Mai Hai-teh)

seeing more commune brigades;
then Wilfred† coming and we writing together
on cool autumn mornings of the China we knew.
Autumn ending, and to Kwang Hua county
the old Lao Hu Kuo of China's history,
seeing what is being done with the waters
of the great Tan Kiang reservoir, which
gives so much power to the new Hupeh.

January 1974, and to hospital, operation and
slow recovery, but thanks to
good doctors and good care able to get
around again; and so in spring go down
to the pottery centre of Ishing by
the broad Taihu Lake, and then
down to Shanghai and out to Fenghsien
where tens of thousands of ex-high-school
youth work together reclaiming
alkali flats by the sea coast for
the Glittering Star State Farm.

Summer to Hui Hsien in North Honan
where road and irrigation work amaze
and an ancient land has become a new
and dynamic one; spirit turning to
matter in no uncertain way; then while
at Peitaiho that year, out into
Tangshan counties, seeing Yangshan,
a brigade that was the poorest of the poor
now with five hundred trees per person.

Came autumn, and we followed the
changing leaves down into Chekiang, on
through Lishui and Lungchuan, where
the She people dwell, where ancient swords
are still made and Lungchuan celadons
the wonder of the ancient world, were created.

---

†Wilfred Burchett

17

From Chekiang on through Pucheng
in Fukien, going on to Kienyang
near which lie the ancient kilns
where Kien-tze tea bowls were made
a millennium past; then on to Nanping
and down the Min River to Foochow
where fine lacquer-ware is made,
and delicate stone carving created. We see
the ancient foundation of Kushan amongst
its mountain forest, Mawei in the
estuary, the great bridge over the
Wolung River, and a new city filled
with light and passion
for the new day. Up to forested
mountain ranges where lies the town
of Tehua, home of the incomparable
"blanc de Chine", then down to
Chuanchow, a thousand years ago the
greatest port in the world; walk
through the pagoda-studded courtyards
of Kai Yuan Ss, then go on to
Tsangchow with its massive irrigation
works; armed militia chanting "Taiwan
must be liberated", a slogan heard
all over Fukien; then we go to Amoy
with Quemoy Island sulking in its harbour,
still under the thrall of the occupation
on Taiwan province. A trip into
the old revolutionary areas of west
Fukien, where so much was started
that now has come to fruition; then
on the new airline from Foochow to
Shanghai, going out to Tsinpu county to see
the fishing commune at Ting Shan Lake,
a group of folk who have come up from poverty
to plenty in no uncertain way.

A quiet winter in Peking, then as
blossom began to show, to the

model county of Pingu, and so on
to that of Paodi in Tientsin, where
lies the heroic brigade of
Hsiao Ching Chuang. And there on
slept in a good warm k'ang* again.

I had visited the oilfields of
Yumen, and Karamai, and now came to
those at Takang below Tientsin, and
the great Shengli in Shantung.
Chinhuangtao now an oil port, with
black gold coming down by pipe
from Taching, then going on to Peking's
refineries.

Early summer, and from
the quietness of Chin Ss temple at
Taiyuan, we went south to see
humic acid fertiliser being made
at Hungtung, then over the mountains
and through the forests of Liu Liang
Shan, to Hsiangning, and Chi Hsien,
two counties that are halting the
flow of silt into the Yellow River;
and there one saw new forests, new
terraced fields, and a new people.

On to Hsiyang, and looking at
the wonder brigades of Tachai, that
have done the impossible, and
made so much from so little, all
by their own efforts. Then with
the hot days coming in, to Peitaiho
again, with papers and typewriters,
looking forward to new journeys
to unfold in the days to come.

---

*k'ang: Bed of mud bricks which can be heated in winter.

Now along the beaches of Pohai Bay
each commune has its fishing brigade,
today with motorised trawlers which go on
out into the Yellow Sea, at times
selling their catch in Shantung harbours.

And sitting in quietness, looking
over rich orchards, and down to the sea,
I think of how in these years, peoples
do begin to draw closer, state
relations with China improve all
the time, as do those between Chinese
and many other peoples, with constant
going and coming accentuated, ever
new bridges being built, making for an increased
flow of ideas, so that old lies
begin to lose their sting, and clarity comes in.

Peitaiho, Hopei, 3 August, 1975

ON REVOLUTION

No revolution that does not
go right down amongst the people,
bringing change to them that includes
liberation from degradation, misery
and exploitation can be called
a real revolution.

There can be an industrial revolution
that benefits a rising capitalist class,
or a green revolution that enables
landlords to oppress peasantry more,
throw more out of work as mechanisation
in the service of landlord profit
comes ruthlessly in. There can be

20

bourgeois revolution that chops off feudalism
and the head of the first King Charles, and
there can be revolution that has
taken the wrong road and ends up
as national chauvinism and social imperialism
which in its greed for world control
becomes the enemy of all working folk.

A revolution
has to reach well into the huts
of the very poor, pull the old mighty
from their seats, change people
as peoples change their environment, with
its ingrained concepts handed down
by priests and politicians in their
own interests; then, and only then
can there be mass creativity with
real emancipation of man and
woman; a start made in down-to-earth
education that fits the needs
of the people who produce all, helping
everyone to analyse, "Why?" and "How?"

And this day when these lines are
written, is People's Liberation Army Day
in China; a day that remembers the
setting up of the armed forces
of the people: working folk
inspired by the ideas that the
Communist Party and its leaders have
brought home to them.
Now with arms in their hands and
dedication in their hearts
making a force which over the
past near forty years has battled
to build a new China, acting
as a reliable supporter
of the continuing revolution
in which all must play their part.

An army that works quietly yet
with deep motivation, strengthening
by its clear example
the hands of working folk everywhere.

Peitaiho, Hopei, 1 August, 1975

ART FOR THE WORKING PEOPLE

Some paint pictures in colours
on fine paper, others with oils
on canvas. There are those who
put their art into woodcuts,
sculpture in ceramics or stone,
and again those who make pictures
with words that can inspire, lift.
Then those who create art with
sweat and farm tools, changing
their scene with each season, making
moving pictures of winds caressing
rich harvests as the ears of wheat
ripen, of bees amongst blossoms,
of white cotton in bloom, and a load
of commune farmers on the trailer
of a bright red tractor, going out
to change the scene again. All of these
pictures made by the people, to which
now are added those of aqueducts
of cut stone, crossing wide valleys,
sturdy bridges leaping over wide
rivers; new electric railways running through
a maze of wild mountains; and in cities
the reflection of fiery furnaces
against the faces of eager steel workers.

Surely there is an art in all the things

people do; the gentle hands of the doctor
attending to patients, the teacher
with wide-eyed children looking up at her,
all wanting to know; in a convoy of trucks
crossing snowy mountains, an oil derrick
being erected on desert lands, terraced
fields, and ships running down the slipways
in shipbuilding yards. Socialist realism
paints many a picture, each one made
more fresh because of people working
together creatively; a picture that
never tires one as do all the degenerate
ones seen on too many western
art gallery walls, where lost artists
record their twisted deadly monotonous
minds in tangled vacuity, into which
viewers try to read some mad meaning.
Little wonder since such daubs are painted for
a special audience that can pay, and
are part of a social system
where the main drive is profit and fame.

Today I saw a schoolboy
sitting by the shores of Pohai Bay
painting a child who stood on the prow
of a fishing boat, the wind blowing
back her hair from her face, caressing
her sturdy legs set firmly apart; all
with the afternoon sun glinting on
the water beyond. And the fishermen
and small fry who gathered around the painter
to watch, saw that he had caught
the spirit of the scene, and laughed
in appreciation. Art of the people,
by the people, in the service of the people, art
come into its own.

Peitaiho, Hopei, 3 August, 1975

23

THE NEW GREAT WALL

For two centuries, foreign imperialism
has punched into China's frontiers,
ever demanding: Union Jack in the lead, the
land-grabbing mad Tsars ripping away
the most, and still no end, for their
successors try to outdo their forebears.
Somehow, anyhow, they want to get hold of
more — which is to be expected for
land-grabbing is part of the nature of
social imperialism.

Down through the centuries, it has
been the northern border that has counted.
Today, other imperialisms squat back
on their haunches, while the northern Bear
stands on its hind legs, still snapping
and snarling. And in the meantime
China goes on strengthening its
sure Great Wall, the one that lies amongst
its people, who in true democracy live
and work together to change their land;
building people full of character, full
of determination, charged with spirit, yet
quiet and modest withal as they work in
units, draining swamps, building dams,
linking up their hinterland with
new railways and roads, and their land
with other lands by new shipping built
at home in the spirit of better service
to all, of self-reliance, and in the
mutual understanding that brings all to
work together; and as
they build this new Great Wall, so do they
give their peoples ever greater, deeper
and more basic strength to meet
all that threatens in the days to come.

Peitaiho, Hopei, 5 August, 1975

Chu Nan, Shantung 1977. Commune children welcome Rewi to their concert.

May Day, 1977, at the Summer Palace, Peking.

Yi children in Kanlo, Szechuan 1977.

Shansi: A peasant mother and children.

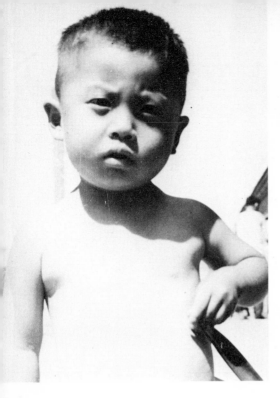

Taching, Heilungchan: This two-year old getting some summer's sun is the son of an old Sandan boy who is now a Taching oil field worker.

Pavilion in the poet Su Tung-po's Memorial Park, Meishan, Szechuan 1977.

So many commune children laugh up at one, Chiyuan, Honan.

Buffalo children, Hsinchow, Hupeh.

RETURN TO TSAI KE CHUANG

Back from the sea of Pohai Bay
lies the People's Commune of
Tsai Ke Chuang, visited once more
after a break of seven years; now
one of its brigades a vanguard
for land reclamation and fruit growing.
Hard to realise that it once supplied
donkey boys who waited in front
of foreign bungalows to take
the city rich down to play on
beaches; where there was
destitution and hunger
each long winter; where children grew up
illiterate, and old burdens
of outworn custom and tabu weighed
so heavily . . .

Then the years of liberation came
in, with heads being lifted and people
at last with a chance to look about them,
even though many still held to old
notions: "Why bother to grow fruit
trees? We will be dead before
they bear." And, "Whoever heard of
the State buying fruit!" But now
fruit tree branches bend low with
their weight of apples, and commune
lasses pack fruit in big sturdy baskets
for shipping by rail. The old swamp
has been drained and reclaimed, and
rice now grows where but fen
weeds once grew. Autumn crops of sorghum
and corn now stand proudly, while
power lines run over fields, bringing
energy to motorised pumps, lighting
up the village. And now in

the warm summer days, with children
away at play, teachers sit
out under trees, concentrating
on the study course they have
set themselves. In all a far call
from the bitterness and destitution
of a rotten past.

Peitaiho, Hopei, 20 August, 1975

FOR OCTOBER THE FIRST, 1975

As autumn winds begin to blow away
summer heat, and October 1975
comes closer, one looks back a quarter
of a century.

Then China lay prostrate. For
the common folk, easy to die, hard
to live. For the elite few,
pampered by imperialist patronage,
soggy with unearned increment,
dull piggish lives, without any
motivation except more profit; served
by a police schooled to delight in
sadistic torture in its sub-human
prisons; an army whose guns were ever
trained on the people. The masses whose
poverty as the years piled on top of
years became increasingly stark; lack-lustre
eyes, big bellies of the diseased, hungry
or overworked children, thin, emaciated
limbs. Landlords who demanded all,
gave nothing but beatings and curses; petty
officials who ever tried to increase their
slice of anything worth taking. Corruption

that crept into every administrative
and business corner, too often
covered with pious phrases, Confucian
tags, or holy words of one brand
or another. Groups that eternally
feasted one another, decked themselves
in silk brocaded gowns.

A time when those who did the hardest
work were dubbed "coolies" and despised
when they should have been honoured.
A rotten old society where in each
and every working home there was
some sad, tragic story.

In northern mountain valleys I saw children
standing numbly, naked in the snow;
the people forced to grow opium, to pay as
taxes; encouraged to smoke it
for solace; prostitutes, some with
as many as seven diseases, living
short, miserable lives; illiteracy
rampant. And all of this, along with
too much more, I had seen with my
own eyes, not once but over many,
many years, ever wondering how long
the people would stand it. Until
from the hills of Hunan, Kiangsi and Fukien
came uprisings, and there grew, too, a leader
who believed in the poor, gave confidence to them,
so that out of their number grew the
armies that made the Long March, which
step by step led on to the liberation of
the whole land from the shackles of
the bestial, chaotic old.

Twenty-six years of struggle
have passed; Land Reform, the Great
Leap Forward, the Cultural Revolution,

and the present movement to study
theory, relating it to the practice
of working-class dictatorship,
have stirred the land to its depths. The
continuing process of changing people
has proved as successful as the making
of the atom bomb, and with much
greater significance. Drugs, prostitution,
along with many of the worst
diseases, have vanished. Prices remain
stable, oil production booms, a network
of pipelines running over great
distances to refineries. New measures
are being taken to boost steel, erosion silt
into the Yellow River is being cut down;
billions on billions of trees
are being planted, millions of ravines
filled with greenery and check dams.
The lessons of Tachai and Taching are being learned
by the multi-millions, whose feet
now move more surely, whose backs
have straightened, with no man bowing
down to any other man. This land
where women cease to be chattels, becoming real
persons with real persons' rights and
responsibilities; where in front of every
child there stretch out new opportunities
to serve the people; where old revolutionaries
have never halted in trying to give all
they can in every way for the cause to which
they have dedicated their lives.

Now a China where the ideas of self-reliance,
of working thoughtfully together, putting
the good of the group above things purely
personal, are seen as a matter of course.
A land where advance is made on so many
fronts, five-year commune schools giving place
to seven, seven to ten, while

28

counties and factories organise and operate
their own universities. Right here in the
Tangshan prefecture where these lines
are being written, a harvest twenty percent
better than the rich 1974 one is now being
gathered.

The peoples of the world today
feel better when China's mercantile
fleets increase, its ships entering
their ports; China who keeps no
troops outside her own land; whose
answer to nuclear warfare threats
is the proposal that the world together
dumps the lot. China who stands
sturdily on her own borders, refusing
to be intimidated by social imperialism
which ever struggles to encircle her.
China the true friend of all peoples
who work for the better world to be.

Peitaiho, Hopei, August, 1975

PEKING RETURN

West winds start quietly
yet irrevocably begin
to blow autumn in; the brush
of time is already painting
new images over old memories.
Yet the magic of that last swim
out into the wide, calm ocean,
with all the sense of freedom it gave,
is still with us. As bags were
being packed, Grandfather Wang
moved down the verandah, watering

29

pot in hand, tending flower pots
and murmuring, "Another year gone!"
Then were we left to the evening
with the sunset lighting up Chieh Shih
mountain as we took a walk, returning
for the nine o'clock news from Washington:
a Nigerian student in the U.S.A. was shot dead
because police thought he was going to a rally,
which he was not; more floods and destitution
in India; more moves and counter-moves
in Portugal and the Middle East; more
vituperation of China from Moscow — but one
can at least be grateful that the horror
bombing of Indo-China has stopped, though
who could feel reassured by the bellicose
speeches coming out of South Korea?

A world in change, with so many
in proud western lands wondering
what kind of a future their children
will face; lands where those who
have cornered their little pile
breed children who just live for fun
and games, with little idea of
the necessity of developing
creativity; lands where the great mass
are caught up in a grim rat race.
Then there is the Third World, struggling
to get on its feet, while over all
the lords of the two superpowers
talk detente, yet ever plan
confrontation; social imperialism
building two nuclear submarines each
month, but still having to buy
grain heavily to feed its own
people; intriguing to gain
new bases, new footholds . . . . .

Amongst the haves, who feel

30

that the old order has given them
all they have got, and much more
than their fair deal, there is grim
determination to hang on to it
at all costs; learn nothing; drop
nothing; blissfully closing eyes
to stark reality; as the situation corrodes,
inflation rises — still they feel secure
in the comfortable homes, clean
cities, and with their special position.
Yet bombs explode in Ireland, Lebanon,
and even London; race riots break out
in Kentucky and Boston, too. Dope
pushers, bank bandits, muggers all
infiltrate, all portents of chaos
with a host of problems that can
but be solved by massive change.

Peking, 10 September, 1975

IN THE SPIRIT OF JOLMO LUNGMA*

In China today
just as Tachai is taken as the model
for agriculture, Taching for industry,
so the struggle for the climbing of Jolmo Lungma
is made an example for sport to emulate.

What a flood of memories
surged in as one watched
the march past of around ten thousand
athletes, of thirty nationalities,
representing provinces, hinterland
regions, coastal cities, Tibetan,

---

*Also written Qomolang-ma Feng (Mt. Everest).

31

Uighur, Mongol and Chiang, along
with Han brothers, and including
those from the province of Taiwan!

Who could have thought three
decades past, that each area
could send in so great a flowering
of working youth to compete
in friendship together, or that
old Peking, now new Peking, could
receive them and proudly show them off
to folk from around the world;
all with so vast a spread of colour,
so great a richness.

With flowing precision Peking's youth
gave displays of their art after
the march past, and one felt how well
the people have taken on the dignity
so much longed for in the old days
of deprivation and chaos; all we saw now
being accepted as the way things
should be; splendid limbs moving
with grace and beauty, so that
the big stadium burst into long applause
as each highlight was reached.
Sections of People's Army and militia
showed their élan and skill; children
ran in with flowers.

And then with the sunset
lighting up the Western Hills
we went back to the city again,
filled with satisfaction
that such a demonstration
from the once poor, denied
and oppressed, could come to be.

Peking, 12 September, 1975

A NEW GREAT CHANGE TO COME

October the First, 1975, and at
the old Summer Palace of Peking
ten thousand banners stream
as the masses flow around Kunming Lake
and hillside courts; people who
include those who have come down
from the great meeting on agriculture
at Tachai, where three thousand
seven hundred delegates from every
part of the land have been meeting.

Tachai, where a handful of poor
once despised peasants changed a strip
of arid loess hill land into
a neat farm giving ample livelihood
to all, as well as carrying out all
responsibilities to the state;
re-housing themselves, spreading
the better way to all communes and
brigades around them, so that their
whole county of Hsiyang changes.

Now have the struggles of the old
exploited come to full victory
as the whole conference decides
that all counties over China
attain the status of Hsiyang'*
enlarging the basis for mechanisation,
bringing more smiles to tough, hard-working
faces the wide land over.

Little wonder, then, that on this
holiday the people rejoice,
children dance, and the world
of working people looks on approvingly.

Peking, 1 October, 1975

---

*Hsiyang county of Shansi, agricultural model county.

33

What is the China you talk about to us?
We're sitting pretty, walled around
by the sea! Let's stay that way!
What has the business of poorer nations
to do with us? We're secure, can
vote out any government — maybe — that
does not accede to our wage demands!
We do not like too many people with
different skin tints from our majority
anyway. What we do concerns us alone!
Here's the pub, mate, let's have a drink!

Monopoly which controls
workers' lives, it seems so casually,
listens and applauds. Nothing scares it
more than any suggestion of international
working-class solidarity; nothing irritates
it more than to hear about the quarter
of the world that has stood up, doing things
without its direction, without its rake-off!
Getting oil, making steel, mining coal, growing
all the grain they need, and building a new
people in the doing. That, of course, is
just what the decaying order of both old
and new imperialisms does not want, and so is
right out, secret services to the fore, to
prevent the idea from spreading.

Over the past half-century
some of the dirt of racism
has been cleaned from the thinking
of the ordinary working man, but
just as bad taboos have to be
discarded in places where they have
been burdens for too long,
inculcated as chief supports

34

for a rotting social order, so
whenever they block advance, have they
to be continually hacked away
from the consciousness of the people.

To the standard bearers of the vanguard
the backwardness of old thinking
is not a matter for too much concern, for
minds are clear and free and all thoughts
given to the study of the way forward.
No one plans to export revolution
which can only come if people themselves
demand it; yet in lands sunk in comparative
wealth, old vestiges weigh heavily;
remnants of the arrogance and contempt
that are self-destroying, still remain
amongst those who have lost the capacity
to learn; so that from the advanced
comes pity for their backwardness
and the smugness that so deceptively
leads to a clinging to feelings
of superiority, as they play with
the gadgets built from Third World
raw materials, that an affluent society
bestows on its followers, though now
with somewhat lessening liberality.

The good earth needs fertiliser
to raise crops; crops need sunlight
and water; those who struggle
for revolutionary change need
the warmth of working-class internationalism
and the rich example of what
working folk in control can really do.

The China whose success
becomes a necessity for all peoples
who demand change, is now the trail blazer
for working people; a land ever more sure

of its destiny, putting theory into
action, testing, experimenting
and succeeding in social advance
with a host of lessons already learned
available for all with commonsense
enough to tune in, to stop for a moment,
look and listen; a quarter of the world
open to study, freely sharing experience
in building, not out to take over
other lands, but ever determined to strengthen
the base of its own society, and show
still more clearly what
the hope of the world can be.

Peking, 4 October, 1975

ON WORKING CLASS
INTERNATIONALISM

All over today's world, peoples
mass to demonstrate, but still
cries come from smashed-up
children, helpless old folk,
as explosions rock city streets
and superpowers produce ever more
multiple-headed warheads for nuclear
missiles; so that fear creeps
into many a home; making one realise
that only with a powerful
working-class internationalism can true
world peace be gained, and the
collection of devil weapons in the
hands of one imperialism or the other
be pitched on the scrap-heap, allowing
all peoples to push ahead to their true
destiny. This is no pipe dream but sheer, downright
necessity.

To foster a sincere and active
international spirit, the teachings
of imperialism, neo-imperialism,
feudalism, great-power control,
along with the remnants of primitive
emotions, heritage of the stone age,
sham sacred encrusted taboo,
irrational thought and shallow
superiority, have all to be resolutely
cast aside: you cannot love a lord
and meet other peoples on a basis of
equality; chauvinism, and like excreta
of racism, must be halted at all costs.

Peoples everywhere, whether snow-white,
rich black, or of any other shade of skin, or
whatever their outward physical difference,
are just people, with no special claim
to privilege or deference accruing.

In China, revolution has brought
Uighur, Mongol, Tibetan, Miao, Yi,
Tai, Korean and Chuang, along with
all other minorities of hinterland
hills and valleys, together as comrades
with the majority Han all turning
away from the disease of chauvinism.
Here then is the beginning of a
flowering international spirit, which
now throughout East Asia comes to bud
as it does over the great continent of
Africa, despite the rattle of police rifle fire
on South African city streets.

Granted, some people because of
great opportunity, do have special
attributes: the scientist, the surgeon,
the clever makers and creators; those
of vision and ability; but for all such

37

in the end there remains no way except
to put their talents into the
service of the people, unselfishly,
should we wish to accelerate
progress away from holocaust
and towards the one world of our dreams.

Now, if the civilisation of which we
proudly boast, is to carry through,
it must set out to find ways to change
the minds of people from grab to give; from
seeing but one's own virtues to an appreciation
of the good points of others; tearing down
class divisions, changing bad systems,
making human exploitation a thing of the
dirty past, forging a strong base for
working together, so that the nightmare of
world war and mass extermination fades into
oblivion.

Internationalism amongst the workers of the world
grows like some improved strain of corn
bearing ever more richly; like a sturdy young
tree, smothered by weeds at times, yet ever
springing to life again as it spreads to every clime;
encouraging peoples to push on, uncover nature's
secrets, a whole universe becoming their own.

Peking, 5 October, 1976

LONG MARCH EXHIBITION, PEKING, DECEMBER, 1975

A tall museum hall, folk moving quietly,
and the sun of a winter's afternoon
filtered through high windows.
A white-haired old revolutionary

stands by, listening, while some
of the newer crop, students of revolution,
describe the epic of the Long March,
when poor leadership was changed over
to good, and small numbers, moving with
incredible speed, and using so much greater
a mobility and fighting spirit, outwitted
the encircling enemy. For long months
the armies of Kiangsi, Fukien and Kwangtung
peasants, vanguard of the world's
exploited and oppressed, hacked,
stormed and battled their way over
wide rivers, through forests of
a thousand serried ranges, climbing
deserted snowy wastes of rocky mountains,
wading through treacherous swamps, no sooner
winning one battle than fighting another; on
despite the action of one who should have
helped but only stupidly hindered, forward
into the great Northwest to face the flank
of advancing foreign imperialists, fighting
them on until victory.

So much did they give
well and willingly, becoming men
of purpose, their lives given to the
revolution with ever sterner
dedication. Now they fade out
but their spirit inspires those who would make
their land the beacon of hope in a troubled
world.

Peking, 19 December, 1975

IN MEMORIAM — CHOU EN-LAI

Hills over which he marched
bend their heads in grief; rivers

he crossed cry as they flow;
peoples of hill and grassland,
of every nationality, in border lands,
on commune grain fields, in city
factories, fishermen at sea, oil
workers at their rigs and miners
underground, feel tears start
to their eyes as they think
of this one who ever struggled so
steadfastly for them; People's Army men
grieve as soldiers do
when a good comrade falls. He who
was loved by the many, has gone on;
a going that came as so great a shock,
felt the whole world round. He who ever
stood steady as great waves crashed
around him, always the wellbeing
of his people his only thought, giving
of himself as few others have given,
his directness and clarity, dynamism
and charm, bringing sure confidence
and encouragement. A life tempered
into the finest steel, filled to the brim
with ceaseless effort and accomplishment,
his name one that people like to have
linger on their lips; his spirit never
dying, but inspiring the next echelon
of revolutionaries to carry on, turning
an old land into a new land.

Wherever fighting was fiercest, there
he stood; when it was necessary that one
sit in the mouth of the tiger, there
he sat; no mission too tough for him
to take; no sacrifice too great
for him to make, ever following the
leadership of Mao Tsetung. Now a life
so rich in meaning, so full of endeavour,
has ended as it has ended for so many

old comrades, their deeds not forgotten,
their spirit and the freshness
of their memory staying always with us,
urging us forward.

Rest, then, you with a soul ever
restless for the revolution; rest
in the comforting thought of work
well done; rest, for in all the springs
to come good comrades will carry on
the fight you have fought
so gallantly, clear through to victory.

Peking, 9 January, 1976

THE INTERNATIONALIST —
CHOU EN-LAI

In the Workers' Palace of Culture,
once the ancient Tai Temple,
winter trees threw their shadows against tall
red walls, topped with golden tiles; ancient
cypresses stood grandly as they have stood
all through the centuries.

And on a bright January day came the people
of China paying homage to the ashes of one of the most
remarkable of world statesmen in modern times.

And joining them up the marble steps
filed many groups of diplomats and friends
in Peking; Asians, Africans, those from the Americas,
Europeans and Islanders, folk from lands big and
small paying silent homage to this revolutionary
who struggled for the building of a better world.

41

And into Peking poured a flood of messages
from around the globe
mourning the passing of Chou En-lai who had
given so much to so great a cause
and whose memory will last sturdily, sweetly, through
all the winters and all the tempests to come.

Peking, 12 January, 1976

ON TIEN AN MEN SQUARE, JANUARY 18th, 1976

It was a paper flower,
merely a paper flower, white with big
green leaves; yet her old fingers
had fashioned it, making it
a true piece of art, so big
it covered her breast; firmly she held it
in front of her with one hand
while with the other she led a grandchild
carrying a smaller flower, coming
on to Tien An Men Square on the tiny feet
of the other day. And those who
marshalled the ceremony motioned her
to join the line of mourners with
huge wreaths who came from city
factories and streets; and so with
her old face set, she went forward
to add her offering to the vast
bank of flowers. And then from her
I looked back behind to the red and gold
Tien An Men Gate, and seemed to see
the spare, erect figure of Chou En-lai
still standing there as the last decades
have seen him stand, with a little smile
playing around his lips. Then beside me as I stood

lined up a whole school of children
and began to sing the International in subdued
    voices
in memory of him.

Peking, 18 January, 1976

HUANG HUA CHENG

Winter wheat glistened under
the rays of a rising sun; snow
drifts gave fields an edging
of white ermine as we crossed
Peking plains, finally turning
into the rugged North Mountains
over which the Great Wall so incredibly
streams. Here, down the avenue
of history have been so many
violent struggles that none now
knows the count.

And amongst this wildness, all
through the millennia, summer floods
have torn out the bones of mountains,
hurling them down valleys, creating
ever widening swathes of desolation;
rocks, boulders, stones by the billion
pitched as if the floods jeered
at the puny efforts of people to eke
out livelihood from hillsides
that in turn became ever more
bare, ever more desolate as human
enemies joined in to crush the people.

Now only a few decades have passed
since foreign imperialism and its
puppets harried the countryside,

and there arose from out of the ranks
of the poor, a steeled Party, grown
to maturity through long experience,
bringing to peasant homes the clear
understanding that they could resist
the enemy troops backed by local
tyrants, and then to deal
with natural disaster itself.

Here at Huang Hua Cheng, with towers
and battlements of the Great Wall
staring down through the haze and snow,
came the people militant, men and women,
old and young, red flags down the
centre of devastated valleys,
armed not only with the new tools
they have made, but also with
a new understanding of where their
struggle should be directed;
now setting out to do what their model,
Tachai, has already done, making
new grain fields out of chaos, throwing
themselves into the fray to bring
order out of madness, using well their
collective strength that makes
even the mountains around bend low
in submission.

Huang Hua Cheng, Hwai Ro, Peking, 17 February, 1976

E D U C A T E   F O R   W H A T?

I pass a school in a mountain
village; a cold wind blows down
from snowy heights, but youngsters
ruddy-faced march out with shovels

44

to do mass work along with elders
on land reclamation: putting into practice
the idea they have learned of serving
the people with all their combined
strength, as a way of life.

Making me wonder as I watch them
how many lives are lived less fully
in the more privileged portions of
our world today; bright children just
being given the urge to somehow
accumulate wealth others have earned,
as a main priority; how many nice
clean young ones taught to be polite
and pleasing, grow up to become simply
money-grubbers, status-seekers, their
percentage of school drop-outs often
turning into hippies, smelly,
hairy and lousy as their primitive
forefathers were, with no other
urge but to do their "thing" no matter
where that leads; just as the opium smokers
of the old China coast lost themselves
in fantasy and avoided cold reality,
finally winding up as food for
scavenger curs on rubbish tips.

Summertime; we came up a winding road
to a mountain town; cool enough,
yet the youngsters had dug a swimming
pool in the river bed, lining
it evenly with boulders, and thus had learned
to swim; had heard of swimming but
had never swum before, for the old
stream that rushed over stones beside
their homes was too shallow, too swift;
but now they could put on a show, swimming
in orderly formation, each and every
one of them; then diving, playing water

45

polo, so that the old valley was
filled with their shouts of fun,
echoing up amongst the mountain tops.
Together they had worked, together
learned, and now together they showed well-
cared-for bodies, their bright
minds sensing new challenge
in their whole environment.

And again comes a lesson learned
often; that there must be an early
basis for real education, built in,
so that once parent and teacher control ends,
youth itself can find its true destiny in
the lives of the people; not I scratch
your back, you scratch mine, not
gang up and knife leaders from behind
in the fight for power, but ever
holding to the clean idea of making
whatever changes an advancing people
need. Not scamps who buy honours as
if they were just cheap advertising,
but unspoiled humans learning to become
part of a collective leadership devoted to
the basic needs of the peoples
from whom all have sprung.

Dreamers can dream away their days,
poets enthuse, trying to extract
the essence from the things down-
to-earth hard work have produced;
but to get real results much tough
struggle has to be gone through.
To build a revolutionary base cost many
a life; to be first across the Tatu River
meant that others had to die in
that epic . . . A little luxury and some ease
are the perks of old folk who have
fought through; for youngsters

it should be the ability to see
the light in one another's eyes that
will carry each and all onwards
to their goal.

Peking, 27 March, 1976

FOR IDA PRUITT

Ida, daughter of Han
and of the Isles of the Immortals
of Penglai, now herself
the gracious Lao Tai Tai
yet ever as young as she feels
in the spirit that is immortal.

Ida,
good comrade through
the tough years of struggle;
deep and sincere in her love
for the common folk of China
to whom she has given her best
for so long.

Ida,
the good American, the quiet
determined worker for deeper
more lasting friendship
with the land in which she
was born, and still loves.

Ida,
this salute from old Peking
that a March wind I hope
will take to you, bringing
with it the fragrance

of spring blossom in all
its glory, that is your
glory too.

Peking, 11 March, 1976

J. M. — IN MEMORIAM

Hongkong lies quietly under
the sunshine of a southern sea,
then suddenly at times comes
a cold wind, and its tall Peak
is shrouded with white mist.

And I think back over the life,
lived through eighty years, of one
springing from old Hakka stock,
forced to find livelihood abroad;
of his upbringing in England, his
training to be an engineer, then
finding China had no use for such;
learning to be an accountant, and
from then on
ever giving his services to causes
he knew were all-important.

1937, Shanghai in chaos,
and there J.M. worked amongst
refugees. Back in Hongkong
he gave his strength to "Gung Ho"
and the efforts of Soong Ching-ling
who with friends supported
the fighting Eighth Route and
New Fourth Armies; then with
the Japanese occupation came
into the interior, becoming the first

clear, honest accountant "Gung Ho" top
leadership had yet had.

The War of Resistance over,
J.M. returned to Hongkong, travelling
to Peking representing Overseas
Chinese when the People's Republic
was first set up, then ever
afterwards becoming a strength
to all he met who worked
for a new China and her better
relations with other peoples.

A lovely home, so often
filled with the laughter of
much-loved grandchildren;
a spot overlooking the glory
of a great world crossroads
which will miss him, as will
the lonely office desk in
the tall building by the harbour.
The many he helped will treasure
memories of him, friends
grateful for the fact that
he lived and was able to do
so much; for J.M. had become
in a very real way, part of
themselves, their thoughts,
and all they tried to do.

It was a sad day that brought
news of his passing, and yet
one felt renewed gratitude that
he had lived, and had been able
to do so much, so cleanly, so that
none who knew him will ever forget
his trim, energetic figure
that battled on for the things
he thought best, unceasingly.

Peking, 12 March, 1976

FOR HELEN AND SAM

In ancient China there were
often two swords in single
scabbard, one yin, the other yang.

Helen and Sam, two halves
of one sword, that has
put itself to the service
of the people in a lifetime of effort.

Now Helen, still as graceful
and svelte as of hardly
approaching middle age, is to be
seventy this year, and we who
appreciate her fire, her passion
to bring in a better China-American
relationship, acclaim her daring,
her élan.

Then Sam, the sincere, the wise,
shrewd, able and warm, who has
made a legion of friends, gained
the respect and gratitude of more
for all he has been able to give,
his genius bringing back hearing
to many who had lost it.

Sam and Helen, two good
Americans, with whom conviction
leads to action, and action
to much accomplishment, these
lines from a Peking desk
are written with love and gratitude
for all you have done.

Peking, 14 April, 1976

50

AGNES SMEDLEY, IN MEMORIAM

Twenty-five years have passed
since the ashes of Agnes Smedley
were laid in *Pa Pao Shan
amongst those she fought with.

Now cypresses planted then
have grown tall amongst the graves
around hers; the city has spread
coming ever closer to this quiet
spot she rests in; and I think
of this child of the American
working-class, with a strong strain
of Red Indian in her,
who felt for her kind everywhere,
especially in this great land
then under the heel of reaction.

Agnes who well understood
what it was to be cold and hungry,
what it was to be one of the denied,
who early learned what class
struggle was, sturdily fighting
for her side.

Think kindly of Agnes,
think of her emotional strength
which she exerted so effectively on
behalf of her fellow poor and despised.
Once she told how as a child
she loved lighting fires; so much
of her grown life was spent trying
to light fires to burn out the dirt
and rubbish of the old order.

---

*Pa Pao Shan, cemetery for revolutionaries in environs
of Peking.

And now on a late Peking spring day,
so many years after, with long
weeping willow branches sweeping
the waters of the canal beside which
I sit to write these lines, I think
again of her, feeling that she would
understand the China of our day
and its tough struggle forward.

Peking, 14 April, 1976

SINKIANG DANCES

As I return to my quiet
Peking home from Sinkiang,
memories linger: the fire
that burns so strongly
amongst the people there
urging advance; the epic
irrigation networks that
push deserts back. And in
pleasant reverie, I think
of the spirit of the folk
of mountain, plain and desert
oases; smiling at the sound
of their songs which still
echoes in my ears, while my
mind conjures up pictures
of the dancers who express
so much in their grace
of movement; vivid flashbacks
that stay with me.

Perhaps nowhere in our great
world, are there more dancers
among the people of a province

than there are in Sinkiang;
these who now dance out the old
and dance in the new.

Gracefully they sway, with
bare arms stretched high; one
line advances, then retreats,
with another taking its place;
Tajik, Kazak, Dulani, Mongol,
Uigher and Han, all in an
ecstacy of rapid movement, and with
smiling faces; so that looking at them, whether
in Turfan, Khotan or Kashgar,
Urumchi, Kweitun or up in the
grasslands of the Tienshan, one
was carried along by their rhythm
and beauty, right into the Sinkiang
they are building together
for truly they dance
as one for that unity, knowing that in unity
lies unbeatable strength.

Peking, 5 July, 1976

CHU TEH — A TRIBUTE

The sturdy old tree
that has stood against
so many a storm has fallen,
while beside it new saplings
it has sheltered, grow apace.
The boy who walked past
tung trees in bloom on the
Ilung ridges of North-east
Szechuan, went out into
the world, ever learning
and trying to apply it, so that

naturally he marched
into the ranks of the revolutionaries,
making the revolution his very
life, active through all
the rest of his ninety years
in its service, right up to
a day or two of his passing.

Walk softly, comrade, for here
lie the ashes of one who gave
much, a leader with that quality
common folk follow, whose quiet
humility masked incredible
determination and devotion
to the cause of the people.

The fighter enemies offered
huge sums for capture of,
dead or alive, who marched on,
cutting through those enemies
carrying out the policies
of Mao Tsetung he served so
loyally, converting defeats
into victories, sharing the hardships
of the common fighter with whom
he lived and loved; one of the
truly great men China has produced,
whose name will live on down
into future ages.

And now this morning
in the serene majesty of
the Tai Miao, white marble
backed by summer flowers,
as embassies, delegations
and the people file past
his ashes in respect, one
thinks back on a life so well
lived, and all he has brought to be.

Peking, 9 July, 1976

54

PEKING RECONSTRUCTS

Shattered villages, towns and cities
there are this China autumn, and still
maybe the land will have to face more
of such; yet all will be well if
the spirit bred through the years of
change survives; a spirit that says
Never mind difficulty! Let's together
forge ahead!
A spirit that is the true legacy of
Chinese revolutionaries to future
generations, fruit of their passion.

Lightly the long bare legs of boys
the sweet smiles of girls keep time
with the carts they load with rubble
and together wheel out of lanes, then bring
in bricks and mortar to where elders
rebuild so methodically yet so swiftly
so many thousands of broken houses
in just this one city, least affected
of the great disaster area centred at Tangshan.

Who orders them? Why do they work
so well together, spontaneously,
old and young, mothers and daughters,
fathers and sons, through long days and
well into the nights, all through old
*hutungs where once would stand the
mansion of some court official, powerful
landlord, warlord or trader, surrounded
by the tiny homes retainers had to build
themselves from whatever was
available and could be scraped
together.

------
*hutungs: lanes peculiar to Peking.

Then the rich looked out in disdain
from their sedan chairs balanced
on the backs of sweating bearers,
to them disaster usually meaning
cheaper service, and to their overlords
a chance to raise
prices, so that in a world in which
much changed they remained the only
unchanging ones, except that they became
ever greedier, ever more debauched.

Today, the people have changed,
evidence all through the hutungs
of this ancient city coming strong
and clear, just as it is amongst
the streets of battered Tientsin,
the city and counties of Tangshan
where natural disaster has struck
so much harder, yet where incredible
courage and determination have been
so finely displayed; all adamant
that out of this evil thing
will rise a good one, so that there
come smiles to the faces of all again.

Peking, 8 September, 1976

IN MOURNING : MAO TSETUNG

Ever does the old
give way to the new.
A giant of his age accepts
the verdict of life
and passes on, leaving
a people who have started
to think in a new way

because of him; his name
one that down through
the ages will resound
sharp and clear, as peoples
press forward to realise
the oneness of all working folk.

When he told revolutionaries
to rely on the working people
of China, for there lies strength,
he believed in the common folk
of a myriad villages; and spoke
a different language from those
copy-book dogmatists who opposed
him, so that his line won out
as practice demanded it should.

When he threw the challenge
at the people, asking "What
do we live for?" there was started
the process of changing the
nature of man from grabbing
to giving; when he urged self-sufficiency
wherever it could be had, he began
to forge a spirit of self-reliance
that makes for strength; and when
on July 16th, 1966, he swam the Yangtze
he started a whole land swimming, too,
for such was the magic of his example.
Never a Confucian prude and
with a youngster's relish
for old-time stories, he could
make homely comparisons
in the language folk understood;
for, above all, he felt himself
to be a teacher with much to say
on things that concerned the people.
His concept of Marxism, one he had gained
through down-to-earth experience in early

Changsha, Peking, San Wan, Chingkangshan,
Kutien, and in the drama of Tsunyi in Kwei-
    chow,
which enabled him to lead,
through so many struggles,
on to the battle against revisionism,
fought through the sixties
and seventies as the new Tsars
showed their ambitions.

His, a life that will be studied
by students of revolution for long to come;
just those words, "The people's communes
are good!", enough to set
the whole of rural China on the way
ahead, so readily did people
accept his leadership; as they did
when he simply said that the Hai
and Hwai Rivers must be controlled;
or when he called on youth in
the Cultural Revolution to hold
to class struggle, get political
understanding, education and medicine
down to the people; build up the hinterland,
bring in the new.

Workers
the world over,
hearing of his passing
will think of revolution
and Mao Tsetung
two words
one
and indivisible.

Now are his writings of
four decades left to us,
while his familiar form fades
out into the Red Dust, mingling

with the dust of old comrades
who, too, led, while those who
remain continue to build
on the basis so sturdily laid.

Peking, 9 September, 1976

CHINA AND THE CLEAR ROAD FORWARD

The skies darkened, and then
broke clear; the winds of
Autumn drove in; dead leaves
fell, were picked up and swirled
under the wheels of advancing
traffic on Changan Boulevard;
the people turned and smiled
at each other, those who had fought
through the long years of revolution
with complete dedication, stood
and said, "Enough!". For there
has risen a small gang of ruthless
operators claiming the whole revolution for their own,
covering each dirty move with shouts of
rhetoric, the more uttered, the more empty;
their real cause simply to assuage their
own lust for power and privilege in the
style of a bygone social order. Experts
in the art of rotten tricks, dubbing themselves
the only pure and true revolutionaries — all
the names they called old comrades fitting themselves
perfectly — ever using the word "revolution"
to crush revolutionary spirit and the
hopes of the people who now must have the
way forward clearly, definitely in front of them.

59

Now are hearts and hands filled
with the great urge to get down
to the tough task of making all
industry like Taching*, all agriculture
as Tachai*, bringing the revolution new
strength, new virility; science and
the arts giving their fullest, as they should.

Blow, wild wind, blow from the highlands
of Yenan, down through the streets
of Peking; little wonder there are
smiles amongst the many, and perhaps
consternation amongst the more thoughtless,
fooled enough to tie up with arrogance and
greed which called themselves "radical"
though now proved to belong to ruthless reaction.

Dead leaves are swept up and burnt;
Crazily the enemy in his most deceptive
form had wormed his way towards the
seat of power, then when finally unmasked
turned viciously to make a coup,
promptly crushed, meeting the fate of
all who try to split and destroy unity:
cast into the dustbin
of history!

As the news spread, and in support
of this new leadership, Peking,
along with sister cities, became
ablaze with joy; the people poured
out on the streets, wave on wave of
them, old fighters, staff and factory workers,
students, army and navy fighters,
sedate old women, laughing children;
banners, drums and clashing cymbals,

*Taching: Pacesetter in Chinese industry.
*Tachai: Pacesetter in Chinese agriculture.

60

millions of marching feet moving
together in determination; through
negative example all have learned
new lessons. Now the future is as
bright as the dawn over the eastern sea.
Peking, city of many splendours,
hub of a vast land with a party
too great to be fooled for long,
a leadership too steeled to let
itself be subverted, or to lightly
abandon its responsibilities. Peking,
city of the future, capital of
a land full of warmth and
hope, true to its destiny.

Peking, 21 October, 1976

OLD   GIANTS   AND   A   NEW   STAGE

Kuo Mo-jo, standing straight,
then Mao Tun; two famous figures
on the literary front, part
of the history of modern China;
listened to by youth over
many decades, now together with
old revolutionary leaders in
the fore once more on the balcony
of Tien An Men, where a new stage
is being ushered in, supporting
the new leadership, bringing
by their presence, old memories
to life again, of struggles
that laid the basis for new advance
to come; welcomed by poets,
writers, artists, sculptors,
playwrights and composers
who will increasingly emerge from

the ranks of fighting folk,
lifting many hearts, stirring
hands to action with their crafts,
strengthening all for struggles
yet to come.

Peking, 25 October, 1976

CHINA AND INDIA MEET AGAIN

Rugged, yellow loess hills —
Yenan four decades ago, when
with a group of doctors,
delegates from the struggling
people of India to the fighters
against foreign imperialism
in China, we stepped down from an
Indian ambulance into a bleak
winter's evening and the warmth
of a welcome by Chinese leaders,
backed by the tough, small faces
of "Siao Kwei"* who crowded
around, eager to take part.

Amongst the Indians led by Atal,
Basu and Kotnis stood,
while with the Chinese group
was Ma Hai-teh . . . Now on another
winter's day in Shih Chia Chuang,
capital of Hopei, here is Basu
again making new history in leading
the first group of his countrymen to
visit China after normalisation of
state relations between the two lands.

------

*Siao Kwei, youngsters attached to Chinese Red Army,
now generally any youngster.

And here again he is welcomed touchingly
by many good old front line guerilla
comrades, together with Ma Hai-teh and
Hans Miller, old doctors on the Eighth Route
Army which spread out on the offensive through
wild mountain lands. Kotnis is here
only in spirit for, following Bethune,
he became the second director of
the International Peace Hospital to
give his life for the cause of China,
and all peoples fighting imperialism.

Today, in this North China city,
a memorial hall has been built to
his memory, a symbol of friendship
between the Indian and Chinese peoples.
Monuments may crumble but the memory of
this pioneer, fighter for working-class
internationalism, will last as long as
the old order exists, and after.
Today pictures of the life of this
Indian have been enshrined here,
along with pieces of documentation.

Around Shih Chia Chuang winter wheat
showed green. There were tall buildings
rising along new wide streets . . . Stubborn,
determined old revolutionary, Wang Ping-nan—
who in 1939 met the Indian group in Chungking
and sent them off to Yenan — amongst those
giving welcome speeches, with Basu replying.

Again China has been in struggle;
again victory has come to her people,
as the criminal gang of camp followers
posing as revolutionaries has been
brought down from power, and a second
liberation has come to the Chinese people,
bringing wide Yenan smiles to good peasant,

worker and soldier faces. At such a time,
for the peoples of India and China to have
this expression of friendship, means
much, for together they do make up
nearly half the peoples of the world, and together
they are targets for seekers after hegemony.

Children swirl in welcome dance,
flags stream in the wind; dust rises
as it rose in Yenan winters.
International Peace Hospital staff
and students of today form a great bank
of alert, cheerful faces. And then
we go on to the Memorial Cemetery,
and wreaths are laid on the tomb of Kotnis —
Atal's and Bethune's too — and so in this
place of peace and quietness comes a
     demonstration
of love and respect to a fighter gone on before.

What a theme to try to weave
words around! How one wishes
that one were a better weaver!
The almost incredible struggle
of the Chinese people who are
the hope of tomorrow, inspired
Basu, Kotnis, Atal, and has
held up Ma Hai-teh and Miller, along
with this poor weaver too; so be it!
The stakes for all humanity are
high! The revolution has just begun.

Shih Chia Chuang, Hopei, 9 December, 1976

THOUGHTS IN THE NEW YEAR, 1977

Snapping, yapping, froth dripping
from greedy jaws, wolf packs
swirl down from winter mountains
driving amongst herds, killing
as they go, then savagely ripping
flesh apart until finally beaten
off by herdsmen.

Cold, crisp, decisive,
a North China New Year brings in
its hope, and problems which
must be faced; staunch
old revolutionaries and those
in support turn anew to assess
and plan; righting old wrongs,
clearing bitterness from many
a heart, preparing for giant
advance in the days ahead.

As better vision is gained, minds
clear. The counter revolution
cunningly masked its intentions
by reiterating "Class struggle
before all else," but down-to-earth
true revolutionaries looked at
the operators who shouted so glibly,
looked and were unimpressed, knowing
well that class struggle manifests
itself in many ways, at times
well hidden before becoming plain to all.

A gang of four infiltrated
leadership, slyly organising
its henchmen at a time of change;
using the excuse of halting
any emerging elite by creating

an elite of its own, which swiftly
began to become a new class
of loud-talking entrepreneurs,
deliberately setting out to make
chaos, to allow for a planned
takeover; even going so far
as to claim that disaster relief
in the immense Tangshan earthquake
was a "diversion", thus
keeping well away from it.

Cunning, deadpan eyes greedy
for their own petty advantage,
contrast with bright, sparkling
ones of the real fighters for change,
who ever give themselves, joyfully.
Details of the vast drama unroll;
exposure of the tricks of this
nasty little crew brings out
in the open one fact after the other.
The people listen, then quietly
amongst themselves, discuss
and assess: the killers have been
driven off, chaos halted, but
the price of peace is eternal
vigilance; this thing has happened,
as throughout history it has
often done. How shall we prevent
it happening again, in
the long years to come?

Peking, 7 January, 1977

NONE CAN FORGET

Over the plains of North China
winter wheat gleams green through

patches of snow. None can forget
that on this January day,
a year past, the ashes of the
well-beloved Chou En-lai fell
over the land to which he had given
his all. I listen to the song
of a great singer telling his story
to an old-time Yenan tune; and tears well.
I see again the long processions
of ordinary folk who came in their
tens of thousands to Tien An Men
in memory of him; quiet, orderly, the
children softly singing as they carried
wreaths, a people's ceremony with
grief on every face; and then I reflect how
ever sweeter the name Chou En-lai sounds
to the many who work to make this land
live up to its promise.

A year has passed. The enemies who in
every way, each and every day, tried
to destroy his work, who behind his back
conspired and lied — these have passed
from the scene, so that the glory of
this true son of the Chinese people shines
ever more brightly, folk still feeling his closeness
and the sense of warm intimacy he ever gave,
as if he still lived and was amongst them again.

Foreign pundits love to dub him
"moderate", and his enemies who
were but empty braggarts, "radical";
yet no Chinese would have called him
moderate when he stood with the workers
of Shanghai in the Great Revolution,
or when he organised the Nanchang uprising;
scarcely moderate when he fought
alongside his comrade Yeh Chien-ying
amongst the hills and streams of East

Kwangtung, right in the vanguard,
as always taking victory and defeat
imperturbably, analytically; no moderate
when he stood with Mao Tsetung in the
great crisis at Tsunyi, on the Long March,
or when he galloped on to the airfield
at Yenan, still in enemy hands, in the face of
a thousand rifles trained on him, to go off
to Sian and deal with captured Chiang Kai-shek.
The only words which could have described
his administration of China in post-liberation
years would have been "brilliant, revolutionary,
and completely down to earth", each
success enabling a bigger step to be taken.

Chou En-lai, people's leader, who
ever held clear in his mind
the needs of those he fought for;
with superhuman efforts struggling
in times of stress to bring leadership
together, so that his land could hold
to progress; his whole heart burning
for those who worked to build; his
whole spirit fighting for them; his
love for them expressed in service
to them, and in his common touch;
he in his modesty and plain style
of living an example to all, his spirit
of internationalism a world beacon.

Not for nothing do the Chinese
people call him "well-beloved",
for on the heart of each and every one
he has left his mark, indelibly. And
so do I close my eyes for a moment
and seem to see his gallant trim figure
so clearly, distinctly, bracing up to solve
a new problem tirelessly and with incredible
devotion; a devotion that still endears him to

those who continue making the revolution,
bringing greater fullness to the lives of all.

Peking, 9 January, 1977

NEW CHALLENGE

A Peking mass meeting is like a sea,
swiftly flowing, at once silent, then
breaking into movement again: on the balcony
of Tien An Men, showed the good, strong,
determined faces of old revolutionaries
once more in the lead, framed by scarlet
banners that streamed in the wind; below
the spot where he so often stood, the big
portrait of Mao Tsetung: in measured terms
the Mayor of Peking announced
the appointment of Hua Kuo-feng to positions
the late leader held, and in steady voice
denounced by name those who had made a
wild bid for power
and had failed; those who had held back
the nation's economy with divisive tactics,
ever distorting the people's culture,
debasing it, fixing it at a level
unworthy of the great people it should serve.
Speakers from all other main sections of
the people followed, the line of drummers
beat in joyous abandon, massed bands played,
the sound making the huge red lanterns with
their golden tassels, sway in unison.

The faces on the balcony were a study
indeed; the old ones with a lifetime of revolution
behind them, Yeh Chien-ying, Wang Chen, Hsu
    Shih-yu

69

and others; for them the revolution
and only the revolution, all the way through;
and there beside them one seemed to see the
shades of so many other gallant ones who
have already marched on, Chen Yi, Ho Lung,
Chu Teh, Tung Pei-wu, and all the rest,
while amongst the faces of the present
the calm, steady one of Teng Ying-chao,
wife of Chou En-lai, by her side another
widow, whose husband fell to enemy fire.
Chou En-lai whose memory remains sweet
and fresh, his quiet smile still giving
confidence as it did all through the
bitter days of struggle.
For these two the people have
an ever-growing love and respect:
Chou En-lai, Teng Ying-chao, two
students jailed in 1919, married
in 1925, ever true to the revolution,
and each other; she one of the thirty
women who went from Kiangsi to Yenan
with the Long March; he, after a life
full of service, having his ashes scattered
over the good earth which lies pregnant
awaiting spring.

Red leaves fall; red banners rise;
the people now see more clearly as
the challenge of building an ever
better China faces them. The new leader
smiles, knowing full well that with the power
of the people militant, all as one,
and all working together, brick being
added to brick already laid through the
years since the revolution began, newer
and brighter victories will surely come.

Peking, October, 1976

PEKING WINTER SCENE

To get the feel of real Peking,
Ride your bicycle through the streets
before a winter's dawn; be one
with the mass of cyclists
steadily moving to industry; then
in the suburbs branch off to
agricultural communes where lines
of farm folk spread over the land,
levelling fields, building new
irrigation systems, making highways,
the glint of the rising sun
shining on their tools,
faces down to avoid the cutting wind
that blows starkly across waiting fields.

Then back to city streets again,
now filled with office workers
and schoolchildren. Walk any
afternoon in a park where there is a lake,
watch youngsters skate, some expert,
some learners, the little ones
joyously riding toboggans. Visit
the railway station and look at the streams
of country folk coming in to enjoy
the sights of Peking — palaces, markets,
and of course the zoo; all storing up
these in their minds to take back
and tell of on village kangs
amongst the hills and streams. Good
also, to enter some of the many
small factories of street committees
where just ordinary folk
create so well.

Peking, a tough, hardworking city,
centre of a fighting land, where

no hint of compromise is given, and
despite all problems life forges ahead,
clear into the dawn.

Peking, 24 January, 1977

COMES CLARITY

In the heyday of their sad rule
over the vastness of mainland China,
Kuomintang officials stole
unmercifully, shamelessly, even
while they murdered, jailed, tortured
all of the opposition they could
lay hands on. Their lives were those
of unbridled lechery, while from
their mouths came a ceaseless stream
of words, ranting on about their own
"services to the revolution";
ever spawning more hangers-on of
like kind.

So did a group of these, in clever
disguise, creep into the real revolution
which the people's fighters had
forged so well, cunningly working
to create chaos and mask their drive
for power; putting up a phoney political
line, ruthlessly pulling down old
revolutionaries, making one more
great obstacle for the people
to surmount.

Now, thankfully, have these been cast
from the leadership they usurped,
and the people with one heart set out

to repair the damage done — just as
they have after natural disasters.
Today, shelters built, should more
earth tremors come, still stand, while
underground tunnels go deeper in preparation
for any enemy bomb attack. The people have
    made
their analysis, as they have learned to do,
    demanding
"Who is our friend, who foe?", their voices
ringing unmistakably clear, with no
hint of acceptance of defeat, no goal
but that of victory.

Peking, 25 January, 1977

VOICES THROUGH THE MORNING MIST

Morning mist in early spring
covers the Peking countryside,
and through it comes the voices
of work teams going out to begin
the day's tasks; a rubber-tyred
cart comes down the hill, brakes
screaming in the long familiar
sound, mules tossing their heads
as they trot briskly, their driver,
a lad of around seventeen, cracking
his whip in sheer exuberance; in
the village a donkey halts and brays,
ducks quack in unison, as they
go in file down to the irrigation
channel that flows so freshly; truly
a homely place is this small
community centre; and from it too

73

comes the chug of one tractor
starting, then another, while
running beside the new machines
come shouting children off to school.

Tiles from an ancient gateway
with temple beside, drop; tall
poplars begin to sprout new leaf;
old Chu who stokes the hot water
boiler rails at old Yang who collects
animal manure for compost heaps, and
both laugh together as only old
stagers who have seen much, can laugh;
women come down to the water
with piles of washing to be done,
their bare-bottomed babies
playing luxuriously beside them,
while a passing visitor halts
by a wall newspaper, marvelling
at what good poets, artists
and writers there are, right here.

Peking, 9 February, 1977

FOR JORIS AND MARCELINE

Again Joris and Marceline
come to China; now almost
forty years since
Joris came first; ever the same
clear-thinking, imaginative
Joris, knowing the score
and puzzling how with his artistry
to tell it to the world
so that people would see better
and hearts beat together.

74

Today in a Peking hall we sat
and saw through three hours
of just one of his films
taken from down amongst
the people, telling other
people gently, tenderly,
how old and young deal
with the things that come
over so wide a canvas in China.

Chou En-lai the well-beloved
who too felt deeply for
the common man, had understood
and recognised a fellow
spirit, so that the way ahead
became possible for good Joris
and Marceline to put their
creative genius into the service
of the millions now influenced
in a way that little else
could have done.

Peking, 10 February, 1977

YET ONE MORE TRACTOR

The feel of steel on cold hands
in winter does not halt youth
that tends machines, unerringly
turning out parts for mechanisation.
Throughout the hinterland new
machine shops work steadily, each
tractor that comes from assembly
lines bringing a lifting of spirit
in the sure knowledge that
increasingly burdens are being
lightened, more credit coming

75

to the revolution, which in turn
means solid victory for all.

No end to the tough times
people can put up with when
in true comradeship together
they realise the importance
of all they try to do! Hardly
a limit to the resources that
can be tapped when the creative will
is liberated, and gets down to the task.

Peking, 12 February, 1977

SPRING FESTIVAL EVE, PEKING 1977

Crackers explode under my window
followed by delighted laughter
as youngsters scamper to another site.
Streets, crowded these last days
with country folk come in for shopping,
have cleared, as the many return
to spend the Lunar New Year
in the traditional way with their
own folk. People smile at each other
even though the northwest wind
blows cold.

Now with the unpleasant "gang of four"
out of their hair, as it were,
relaxation and confidence return,
people understanding still better that
making must go with thinking, practical results
must be the end of discussion; that

nice words alone, repeated too often, are
simply a waste when no production follows.

The great chunk of the world
that is China celebrates the traditional
New Year happily, but everywhere
there is the determination to build a richer life
and make good ideas the basis
for doing more, doing it
better, learning from old mistakes.
People, glad their land has escaped
the tragedy the counter-revolution
planned for it, all generating
a New Year's resolve to make
their world a better place,
to puzzle things out, create;
eyes turned towards the next
quarter of a century with all
the promise it contains.

Peking, 17 February, 1977

FOR SHIRLEY

Lass of New Zealand's
sea-girt loveliness, a bit
of the real Aotearoa, with
its forested hills, wide
plains; a daughter of a builder
of boats, herself builder
of a bridge of friendship
carrying the truth of China
clear into the hearts of
her own folk at home.

Shirley who in the chaotic
period prior to Liberation,
came to Shanghai to get help
right through to where it
was meant to go; Shirley who
when the great change had
taken place, punched the book
"Yo Banfa" through to its first
publication, and then, a quarter
of a century later, reprinted it
for the new generation of her
countrymen, ever showing her love
for the people of her own land
and those of China.

Shirley Barton, true blue, who
makes friendship the gem it is;
who puts theory into practice
carries the load, holds steady
on course, always magnificently.

Peking, 2 March, 1977

FOR JIM WONG

There are different kinds of New Zealanders:
descendants of Scotch, Irish, Welsh, then
of many English counties, sprinkled with
other Europeans; there are the original
folk, the good Maori; then, too, other
Polynesians, Indians, and in every town
the Chinese who have so high a place in
pioneering history. Of these came Jim.

His farmer forefathers dwelt along
the East River of Kwangtung, in

Tseng Cheng county, emigrating clear
of the feudal rule of later Manchus
to find opportunity in newly
settled lands; in Dunedin Jim grew
to manhood, brought up a family, then
finding his main interest in working
for an understanding of China, coming
to Peking to teach English, then
returning home, going on with the task
he had set for himself; coming again
to China as leader of visiting groups,
ever patient and thoughtful, always
servant of the people, whether travelling
with me on lecture tours, or in his Auckland
home, a New Zealander of a new kind,
using understanding as it should be used
to break down ignorance; and I wonder
how many times I have said, "Thanks, Jim!"
and how many times at the end of travel
has he murmured, "Made it again!"

Peking, 3 March, 1977

FOR FLORA AND NAT

Here on a Peking morning with
a March wind blowing, I think
of that cosy little home that too
has been home to me so often;
with garden and lawn behind, where
many a meeting of concerned folk
has gathered under an Auckland sun;
where, too, has been many a frolic
with happy grandchildren. Here
Flora and Nat, despite greying hair,
think and plan, for today it is

79

not only in the luxury offices
of powerful corporations that
the future is calculated;
increasingly the people say
the business of our land is
our business; who profits from work
and why? Who goes abroad to fight
and die, and why? Who toils to pay,
who just passes days in play, who friend,
who enemy? Who sees things that are part
of the warp and weft of good living?
So much have you two discussed
in world conferences, or just together
with friends at home,
all down through the years,
tellingly.

Peking, 3 March, 1977

FOR PIP

Pip, who ever had to struggle,
fight his way through schooling
and win many a stiff tussle after;
full of determination, taking
his stand, with no hint of change,
hanging on despite all; good comrade,
engineer, teacher, brother, and for
Sylvia, good husband too.

In the battle for understanding,
New China helped him, and in turn
did Pip do his best to bring to New Zealand
understanding of the new order
he had found. "Too impulsive", some said,
but how much better than to be
a stick-in-the-mud; more hopeful

to look up at the stars, than ever
down at one's toes. All through
the years his letters, how many
thousands of letters, along with his visits,
encouraging; ever he wondered what
he could do to help, editing, publishing
with slender resources; so that I often
think of him in his quiet home with
flowers around, apples on trees,
lawns of a college campus in front,
backed by Southern Alps; think,
and am pleased with the staunch
image that rises in front of me.

Peking, 4 March, 1977

FOR MANNY

Manny, you of the glorious vintage
of Joe Hill; ever a rebel voice,
veteran in the great fight for
the American working people, one
with those who in 1918 sang,
"They herded us like cattle,
tore us from home and wives,
yes, we've heard their rifles rattle,
and have feared for our lives."

Then, Manny, you and Grace went
to help the October revolution, with
all its promise; later, right in
the darkest days of the thirties,
came to Shanghai to raise the
"Voice of China", which told
people what they wanted to hear about,
the realities of imperialism.

81

The new China came into being
with you in the USA keeping up
the fight to bring more understanding
of China to the American people;
then at the invitation of Chou En-lai,
the well-beloved, did you bring folk
to China to study and to learn.
California, and tragedy struck; Manny
lost his Grace, but later gained Berte,
along with some of her youth and energy.

Rising eighty, yet is Manny still
the practical carpenter, building,
making, keeping in touch with youngsters,
loving them well; still the tough
fighter, marching down the long road,
ever with a warm place in the hearts
of all who have worked with you.

Yes, at eighty, you and I, Manny,
can say such things to each other,
for now who knows how much time
will be left to us to say them?

Peking, 5 March, 1977

RED GATEWAY:

In Memory of Edgar Snow

Little red gateway and
a lake beyond; students
around, and the trees in
full leaf as we came to see
the stone over Ed's ashes.
There was his son, Chris
and his old friend, Ma Hai-teh

who together with him stood
with the people in old
liberated areas forty years
past, and too there was
the seven-year-old Jui-chin
who confided he was going
to be a footballer when he
grew up, and who now held
a bunch of wild flowers he
had brought to solemnly place
by the stone.
One generation passes swiftly
on to the next, but Ed's "Red Star"
lives on, bringing understanding
and respect for the fighters
who fought well then, and still
fight on today. Around us
the red banners of May Day still
streamed, with now the hearts
of the millions moving in unison.

Peking, 2 May, 1977

WHAT DO WE LIVE FOR?

A small, sweet face
upturned to mine,
"Grandfather, tell me,
what do we live for?"

"Why ask me, child?"
I reply, and she says
the teacher has asked her
to bring back an answer
tomorrow; so I counter
by saying, "What do you think?"

bringing the prompt reply,
"To serve the people, that's all!
We learned that right back
in kindergarten!"

Surely, out of the mouths
of babes comes great wisdom;
a lesson for greedy profiteers,
seekers after face, fame and fortune,
one too for
succeeding generations to
think over, work through.

Not for tribe, clan, family,
not for stealing what
the other man has, but for
the people of the world
who create, and would increasingly
do so together.

Peking, 4 February, 1977

PART II

From Hainan to Heilungkiang

AROUND YU TSE

One had come across the Taiyuan
plains to Yu Tse, in its beginnings
as a modern town, when industry
was sprouting amongst the fields
of grain. Today it has become a still
swiftly-growing municipality with tall
buildings, busy streets, and
railways converging upon it; so that
all around there seem to be endless
trains in motion, engines hooting
through the night. However, our halt was made
not to look at industry but to spend
one day in Hao Tsun and another in
Tung Chang Sho, two vanguard brigade
villages that have shown the way ahead; both once
drought-stricken, landlord-ridden, both
now led to new livelihood
by the new day, the new way, their
peasant leaders going to self-reliant
Tachai to learn; ever coming to understand
how there are two lines in thinking,
one only of which leads forward.
These, as they now mechanise, and show
what can be done with village rebuilding,
bring in a new quality to living
that shows up well in the happy faces
of the children around.

Yu Tse, Shansi, 27 May, 1975

FRONT LINE FIGHTERS
AGAINST EROSION

Through the mountains above
Hsiangning, a riot of wild flowers

in gold, white and purple, along
forest edges — old forests now
protected and renewed; then on
down to loess hill farmlands where
now trees fill up eroded valleys
and check dams hold up silt-bearing
waters. On plateaus above
valleys and hillsides, great new
terraces run, with high walls,
like sections of the Great Wall,
encircling well-levelled fields, that
no storm can wash away; all speaking
so eloquently of the cheerful sacrifice
and mighty effort that has
gone into them. Here in these
highlands, so many communes with their own
walnut mountain, each with its ten
thousand trees, ten thousand victories
for the future.

Children's Day, and down from dozens
of villages, across stony valley
riverbeds, the children stream to
commune centres; spotlessly white
shirts, red banners, wide sun hats,
the morning ringing with their laughter
and song. These are the heroes
of the next generation destined to
carry through the task their fathers
have begun, making an old land
into a new land, denying the old
man-eating devil Yellow River
the good soil it has sucked up
through the millennia.

New forests on headlands; flowering
ash filling the air richly with
its scent; the Red Flag forest of
Chi Hsien, Tung Ao in Hsiangning

with orchards beside; people who had
never seen an apple now harvesting
in plenty from their orchards.

Trees, and still more trees!
Hua Shen-teh, aged eighty, straight,
tall and lithe, stroked his thin
beard, and laughed as he looked
over the hillsides green with
the trees he had planted, is still
planting. Here the spirit of change
has taken strong hold, and gallantly
the people respond.

Chin Ss, Shansi, 4 June, 1975

THE REVOLUTIONARY BASE OF TACHAI IN 1975

Then
just a few eroded valleys
with cave homes cut in them
which so often collapsed in
summer storms; scattered
patches of grain fields, and
bare hills above, with a people
ever held in grinding poverty.
This
the legacy bequeathed by
the old order to an awakening
new.
Out from the ranks of the people
rose their own leadership, trusted
and thoughtful, full of fighting
spirit.

Swiftly
hands joined together, in tough
down-to-earth struggle to re-shape
the land they lived from; with
a new spirit in the ascendant
set-backs were dealt with, none
halting the drive forward.

Just a litle group of poor
and middle peasants, amongst
barren Shansi hills, but one
that by its adherence to the right way
has changed their land and their
lives, making Tachai a name
to be conjured with; an example
to be copied all over the land;
a school, a practical research
centre; a spark, a beacon; a
revolutionary base; Tachai
where spirit born of good
theory has so triumphantly
turned to matter: solid, comfortable
homes, rich terraced fields,
irrigation flowing even through
drought years; orchards; highways;
and the promise of so much more
to come.

Tachai, now copied by brigades
far and near, its spirit pervading
country towns and villages, so that
all begin to look anew at their
surroundings, seeing with new eyes
a possible future once not even
dreamed of.

A seed dropped, taking root
in an ancient earth wall; sprouted,
grew and came to flower;

put out runners which struck down
and grew into other plants which too
burst into flower, until finally
the wall was covered with them.

The seed was the thinking that
moved Chen Yung-kwei*, the flower
Tachai; so that now in a changed
countryside so much new has come
to bloom.

Tachai, Shansi, 10 June, 1975

---

*Famed Leader of Tachai and now Vice-Premier of
China.

FOR OLD CADRES

Old revolutionaries look back
at places they struggled in so bitterly
during the Wars of Resistance
and Liberation . . Today they are
middle-aged, or growing old, but
their spirit still carries them
as proudly they say, "Our city
had a fifty percent increase in
industrial production this year; we now
make tractors, and trucks also;
we are carrying through new
irrigation projects all the time!
Each year our grain production
goes up!"

A long call from
the time they went with the lope
of fighting guerillas from village
to village, living with the people,

encouraging them to stand together,
to go on producing while fighting;
giving cohesion through continued
and intense education; always hungry,
ever taking part in the struggle,
one way or another; night marches,
day marches, all just part of the
way things were; wounds, sickness,
cold and heat, part of their
payment for services rendered.

And now
they puzzle with new problems, on
how to go deeper into the political
philosophy that has carried them
so far and so triumphantly . .

Salt of
the good earth of China are these
who apply their experience and
creativity so directly and with
so sure a result.

Chinhuangtao, Hopei, 28 July, 1975

CHAOCHOW

Here once lay a proud city
of landlords, officials and merchants,
heavily garrisoned, where the lord
intendant came in his chair on
the backs of many bearers; and all
seemed secure as Confucians, worshipping
manners, privilege, propriety, held
their sway in the way things were
ordered to be. Potters turned out

fine porcelain for feast tables, peasants
starved, but the granaries of the elite
were ever full. Then further down the coast
at Hai-lo Tong, revolt flamed. Striking
from liberated West Fukien a force
of Red Army men came, so that naught seemed
secure any longer. Landlords came to terms with
the Japanese aggressors, then with the following
Kuomintang.

But finally the people,
held down for too long, took over, and today
in the old Fu Yamen, six thousand representatives
from all Chao An county, meet to discuss
how to implement new agricultural policy
decided on in the great meeting at Tachai.

When working people take charge, and the old
is truly demolished, all can be done,
one success laying foundations for the next.

Chaochow, Kwangtung, 31 October, 1975

SWATOW EVENING

In the west a setting sun
throws the hills around into
a red haze, reflecting its light
on the beautiful form of a lad
unclothed but for briefs, who
poles a boat in the harbour below
my window. Then as darkness deepens
lights come on over ships lying
at anchor, and in from the sea
fishing junks, brown sails set,
glide quietly. Here once was but

93

a small fishing port, then later on
for foreign traders; now in this day
become a growing industrial centre
whose products go into the far
interior, as well as abroad.

Still Swatow womenfolk make fabulous
embroideries, though now receiving
full fruit of their labour. Swatow,
a city backed by a rich countryside, an
ever-changing city from which
many a poverty-stricken emigrant
once sailed; and to which he or she
now came back to catch up with
changes in thinking, and all that
grows from such.

Swatow, Kwangtung, 2 November, 1975

KWANGTUNG AUTUMN

Out to Peking airport, early frost
white over green fields of winter
wheat; tall poplars lining the highway
like golden columns; children carrying
haversacks and water bottles, out on
a route march. Then the warmth of friends
who came to farewell before we rose
over clouds down to Kwangchow, still under
tropical sun; trees that had been felled
in the last typhoon, propped up
erect again, with branches pruned.

Afternoon, and a gentle rain fell
while below my room came the sound
of bare feet in sandals, lightly slapping

the street as youngsters trooped home
from school, the lilt of their voices
rising to the Flower Pagoda, which
looked down on them encouragingly
as it stood so regally over trees around —
just as it has stood down through
the centuries, weathering a thousand
typhoons.

Kwangchow, Kwangtung, November, 1975

KAOBI

A wide river with engined tugs
that chug as they pull lines
of boats upstream; rounded hills
with more hills rising behind them;
an afternoon sun painting some slopes
bright, others dark. On my desk two
lovely porcelain pen holders with
guerillas painted on them in pastel colours . . .
Once too, these hills were alive
with fighters for liberation, as lean
and barelegged as the farmer who
carries out manure to vegetable plots
below where I write these lines.

Kaobi in Tapu country, a place of vivid
contrast where people now use waters
and set up hydro-electric plants,
lighting up their villages, and beginning
to fire pottery kilns. Steadily they
build more and more highways, smilingly
pick bananas from under the fronds
that give shadow to fish ponds; clatter
along on tractors with trailers that

raise the dust as they go to and fro
bringing in kaolin for the big kilns.

Kaobi, set like a gem amongst the hills,
from which will arise, as the spirit of its
people grows in strength, new wonders
for a world to marvel at.

Kaobi, Kwangtung, 5 November, 1975

LO DUNG IN FO KANG

Once they were forced to grind up
rice husks to make a coarse meal, pick herbs
from the hills to go with it, fight
for livelihood with carrying poles
biting deep into bare shoulders, as
they staggered over hill tracks to carry
charcoal down to the plains to keep
the rich a little warmer in the winter.
Because they were poor, the weight
of the old society fell heaviest on them;
because they spoke only Hakka, others
around did not understand them; for them
it must have seemed that every man's hand
was against them, as they huddled together
in their high valley huts. Then came
change and the old order was overthrown
so that suddenly they found that they
were looked on as valuable people
and that they had power, with all the old
riffraff being swept away.

So did they
turn and re-shape their valley, burn
tile and brick, build homes, a school,

a clinic, then harness hill streams
to give their hands more strength, build
a highway so that their tractors could
haul trailers of produce out, and what
they needed in; learning of Tachai, then
copying it, now together ever finding
new ways ahead, so that the old mountains
look down, and the streams that glitter
in the sunlight look up, all smiling
encouragement to these folk who
have taken over their own so exultantly.

Lo Dung, Kwangtung, 24 November, 1975

THE GREATEST EVENT OF OUR DAY

To a world engrossed in aspects
of superpower rivalry, events
in the one quarter of the world
that is China seem remote at times.
An item about a new Chinese oilfield
or a Chinese satellite in space, command
momentary attention; but then again
minds turn to Lisbon, Luanda, Beirut,
and the grim game of check and counter-
check being played out there; the latest
on the New York Stock Exchange, or how
the bankruptcy of New York is being
staved off, for isn't that city the centre
of the whole capitalist world?

How few realise the change that will come
when ten million machine tools already
spread out over so vast a land as China
set out to make more machine tools,

hundreds of millions of better implements
for communes, their brigades and production
teams? Or when five hundred million pairs
of hands start to double big crop results
already gained, reclaiming, irrigating
immense tracts of wasteland, hillside and swamp;
or when the fire of doing things to copy
Tachai spreads to people in city
shops, offices and schools, so that
there comes still greater intermingling,
everyone with a clear aim, definitely set;
none thinking in terms of superpower
glory, but simply with the ideal of getting
rid of backwardness, bringing in the strength
of mechanisation, lifting more burdens
from shoulders that have carried them
too long; so that all drive forward into
the future, full of confidence that what
they say they can do, they will do.

So does this vast movement of working
people gather momentum, from Tibetan
highlands down over the central plains,
from river deltas to Northwest grasslands,
great deserts to sea beaches, an immense
thing of a whole people on the move; one
that started simply enough in a tiny village
amongst Shansi loess highlands, but now
in its implications, becomes the greatest
single happening in our world today.

Kwangchow, Kwangtung, 27 November, 1975

SHANGHAI AND TACHAI

Once Shanghai imported raw materials
then exported finished goods, made

under every abuse workers could be
forced to suffer; in counties around,
children were big-bellied with
blood fluke, ever hungry, dying
quickly. Now, less than three decades
after the great change, the movement
to copy Tachai activates a whole
countryside again, so in Chuan Sa,
Nanhui, Sungkiang, Kinshan, Kading,
Paoshan and the rest, evidences
of how advance is being made show
clearly. In the Sinwu commune, once
just a semi-deserted swamp, I pause
near three old-stagers sitting by
a new pumping station, and we exchange
smiles; then talk to a sixty-eight-year-old
woman quietly at work with rice sheaves;
laugh a while with children from
the brigade school, noting how with all
of them lies so great a satisfaction
with their chosen way ahead.

All around old Shanghai there is change.
Now no longer does the Whangpoo River
divide, for an underground tunnel and
two bridges will increasingly bring
the two sides closer together.

At Kading, industry and agriculture
interlock; whitewashed walls and
quiet canals there still are; there too are
locally-made tugs pulling lines of
reinforced concrete lighters; fields
are bright with coloured flags as
city cadres and workers help farmers
to level the land, Tachai style.
And a small memory remains with me
of two small girls, legs hardly long
enough for feet to push the pedals of the bicycles

they rode, yet each bicycle pulling,
from a commune road out to the highway,
a trailer loaded high with white cabbage
for the market — the short braids
on each girl's head swinging as they
turned laughingly in banter to each other.

Today's commune of Shanghai, with its
urge to follow Tachai, and its growing
variety of tasks, presents a new
problem in energy conservation,
forcing new mechanisation; here now
one sees machines for picking
seedlings from rice beds,
then to deliver them to mechanical
rice transplanters. These, along with
a whole range of better farm machines
show the strength and creativeness
of the Shanghai worker, now at one
with the peasant in their march forward
together.

Shanghai, 5 December, 1975

ON VISITING THE HSIANG FEI TOMB AT KASHGAR

She was spirited, beautiful,
capturing an Emperor's love,
gaining the hate of other
Peking palace ladies; even in
the traditional style of her
people carrying a knife to protect
her honour, yet a thing against
palace law, which brought her
before the Dowager Empress's court
while the Emperor was absent, and

100

the cruel sentence she should
forthwith hang herself.

It took her three and a half years
to be brought to Peking, and
the same time for her funeral train
to return home again over deserts,
mountain and plain.

They laid her under the cupola
of the great tomb of an august ancestor,
her remains beside those of her mother, one
of the smallest of the seventy-two
graves there, but her name now
has become the name of the whole place,
for her memory still shines bright in
the folklore the people love.

Came the People's Government, and
the whole tomb site was repaired,
so that new green tiles now glisten
under the Kashgar sun, along with
green leaves of tall poplar trees
beside; so many old stories are now
forgotten, but this one in its passion
is still remembered.

Kashgar, Sinkiang, 31 May, 1976

CHILDREN'S DAY IN KASHGAR

Who would have thought
that here where the great
alpine ranges of Central Asia
meet, and where in front
of the people lies the greatest
desert of the world, that here

could be gathered so lovely
and colourful a bunch of children
as those we moved amongst in
a Kashgar park on Children's Day.

Here were children of different
skin tints and eye setting,
mingling happily as one, some
listening to the concerts of song
and dance, others playing amongst
the white-barked poplars on
this bright summer's day which
was their day, determined to
live it to the full.

Soon these will grow to join
the ranks of working folk, fighting
for basic principles and self-
reliance in various fields, showing
how much the unity of child life
can continue and all streams
flow together into one, carrying
a message over snow-covered peaks
out into the world of working people
everywhere.

Kashgar, Sinkiang, 1 June, 1976

SINKIANG

Modern highways lined with straight
poplars, shooting skyward; an expanding
capital, a newly awakened countryside, thirteen
peoples who ever forge unity, no longer
looking on one another as enemies.
Once Tsarist Russia sent in troops,
Queen Victoria tried to set up

102

Yakub; US imperialism thought
to make Osman of Altai head a
buffer state; and then after
its liberation, the new Tsars
conspired to raise rebellion
amongst the Kazaks. Imperialism,
in all its various forms, never
gives up trying, one way or
another, to gain control of this
now reviving garden of Eden.
From here in the very remote
past so many peoples went west to
lowlands, so many east down
the Kansu corridor. This land received
in turn as the millennia slipped past,
revolutionaries, technicians, workers and
farmers from the interior, coming together
with peoples who have struggled so long
for the better livelihood
now at their door.

Urumchi, Sinkiang, June, 1976

CHIRYIA

Here against the communes
of this county called Chiryia in Uighur,
Tse Lo in Han, sands of the Taklamakan
beat unmercifully, like the waves
of some vast sea, trying in its great
storms to turn all it touched to waste.
Then came a new spirit amongst people
who farmed oasis lands; fired by it
they went out over the Gobi waste,
bringing down Kunlun rivers that
had been flowing underground uselessly;

103

under the blazing heat of summer
and the freezing winds of winter
taking water out to the communes
that fringed deserts, so that now
four lines of trees rise green
along new canals with water rippling
along their stone-lined sides; sand
hills are levelled, more trees planted;
wind breaks change wind direction,
new crops, new orchards. Canals, trees,
reservoirs, then more electricity
to operate pumps; one comes after the other as
the battle front surges on, out to do what
savants deemed the impossible.

Tse Loh, Sinkiang, 8 June, 1976

K H O T A N

From here through the centuries
has come the best jade.
Innumerable craftsmen all over
China have fashioned it into
living art; from here too silk
and rugs have gone out over
incredible passes, down into
the sub-continent. And to this place
came a form of Buddhism that
took root and blossomed in China,
Korea and Japan.

Now busy farm folk no longer
mull over the glories of a forgotten
past, rather do they speed the construction of
canals, conserve mountain waters in
reservoirs, fight back at the vast

desert that would ever overwhelm, as
in the past it buried so many cities.

Old industries for rugs and silk
become new, modernised ones; trees
are planted by the million, while
ever more grain comes from better
harvests, and an awakened people
struggle for the peace and plenty they surely
after long ages of chaos, deserve to win.

Khotan, Sinkiang, 9 June, 1976

TURFAN

Pity the old monks who
agonised in the caves of
the Fiery Mountain, after
they had crossed so many deserts
searching for a way of life
through holiness and suffering,
but in the end leaving nothing
but painted cave halls that
foreign adventurers, academic
or official, out to grab,
looted at will, gaining some face
amongst their kind in the process.

Wars surged over Turfan, just
as desert sands did; ever the people
grew poorer; the rich gathered up
their spoils and fled, until at last,
riding on the East wind, came a new
force, devoted to the service
of the people and sacrificing all
to give it; so that down in the hot

oasis of Turfan its impact sparked
immediate change, old irrigation
courses were made effective, new ones
built, wind breaks planted, and with
grape vines spreading everywhere
the people smiled; grain and
cotton fields grew ever richer and
people became, as never before,
masters of their own fate.

Turfan, Sinkiang, 12 June, 1976

K W E I T U N

The tar-sealed highway glistens
under the fierce summer sun,
as it shoots over Gobi waste,
grasslands, then through extending
cultivation. Finally we turn off
from the Ili road and are in Kweitun,
new capital of the Kazak area of Sinkiang.

Tall, quiet men greet us gravely, yet
warmly. Our comrade Mohammed who has
travelled so far with us, is glad to
be home again; over the radio come
honeyed words from across the border,
lauding peace and progress, when actually
something entirely different is in the minds
of the new Tsars who ever plot how to
smash what has been built up in China;
but on the China side of the border,
memories of so many incidents at Ili,
Yumi and all the rest that will not
be so easily erased.

Morning in Kweitun: the sun glints

106

on the leaves of tall poplars outside
my window, white bark contrasting
with summer green. Kweitun, a new town in
      construction,
centre for people of mountain and plain,
out to tame the wilderness and through struggle
change all again.

Kweitun, Sinkiang, 16 June, 1976

WUSU

Not easy to become a Tachai county
anywhere; but here in western Sinkiang
it must have been tough at times
to give the various peoples who
have come together, both pastoral
and agricultural, the understanding
that raises the spirit to dare and
to sacrifice, spending strength liberally
to gain new livelihood for all
which in turn brings in
new freedoms.

Wusu, a county that rises on
the remnants of the old and the decayed,
that looks over the broad waste of
land that surrounds it, and sets out
to reclaim more and more of it,
bring water to it, afforest it;
get the common folk to see that their
future is not desperate and hopeless,
but one filled with promise and cheer.

And up in the high, cool valleys
of the Tienshan, Wusu has its pastoral farms,

with hardy Kazaks herding stock in green
mountain valleys, under tall spruce;
their homes, shops, schools and clinics
all in felt tents that dot the grasslands
white. China's mountain folk
who too help to forge China's destiny.

Wusu, Sinkiang, 18 June, 1976

SHIH HO TZE

Revolutionary armies of the Chinese
people built up a tradition of not
fearing any odds; of complete
devotion to the tasks of revolution,
no matter what sacrifices were entailed.

And in that tradition there came,
storming up through Chinese Central
Asia, the forces of liberation, taking over
armies that surrendered to them,
passing on some of their great
spirit so that together they formed an
army of construction, that set about bringing
life to wild barren lands, making life-giving
waters flow, tapping underground
resources, forging on
with the incredible courage and
stamina of the Long March; working on until
they had the land they settled in, desert
or stony Gobi waste, flowering.

And here at Shih Ho Tze they built a centre,
finally after two heroic decades
passing it over, with its great farms,
to civilian authority again.

Through all the years it was not
that they did things for the people,
but rather with them, bringing in
as comrades, families of soldiers,
workers, technicians, students,
who together became the working
people of a new kind of city.

And from Shih Ho Tze did their work
extend, on Ili plains, up in the Altai,
down around the Taklamakan desert, in
all an epic of construction, that
has laid the basis for more of its
kind to come, until all the
wastes of Sinkiang are covered
with crops that laugh back at the sun.

Shih Ho Tze, Sinkiang, 20 June, 1976

U R U M C H I

"City of Beautiful Grasslands",
as the Mongolians had it, and under
the lordly peaks of Tienshan,
once just a small walled frontier
town beside a little reddish
pagoda-topped hill (which
gives its name to a new department
store in the city beneath)
Urumchi now with industry on
the grand scale, serving desert
oases and mountain valleys.
Here a hundred thousand cotton
spindles hum, tractors roll off
assembly lines, students from
the many nationalities of Sinkiang
flock into training schools.

Urumchi, where exhibition halls
tell of so great a progress and where a
museum shows well some of the glories of the
old Silk Road, and tells of Han and T'ang.

Urumchi, that becomes a centre for
China's far Northwest, a place with
much history behind it, where many
good Communists were murdered and where
memorials to their three leaders stand
quietly, still carrying their message
to the generations that arise.

Urumchi, Sinkiang, 22 June, 1976

TIEN CHIH

Many streams flow into this
the perfect mountain lake, just
one bright silver torrent
hurtles down from it, bringing
life to the folk who have
converted waste to farmland
on the plains below. Bogodo Ola
in its everlasting snow, looks
down over tall spruce that
stand erect as sentinels.

We climb up the mountain road.
Kazaks set up felt tents for
midsummer pasturing; sheep string up
the hillside, cattle nose amongst
long grasses by the water's edge.

Many streams, many peoples
of Sinkiang and the whole world

110

that some day will surely flow into one,
bringing all nearer their true destiny.

Urumchi, Sinkiang, 23 June, 1976

YIN KOU

City set by the marshes of
the Liao River estuary. Heroic
city that suffered from so heavy
an earthquake, but in a year
had recovered; its communes
gaining bigger crops than ever,
its factories raising production
still higher; its youth strengthened
by adversity. And now across
the Pohai Sea comes news of a still
greater earthquake in a sister city.
But folk, fortified by their ability
to master the worst, know that
in Tangshan and in Tientsin too spirit
will triumph over matter; and in a year
from now, as at Yin Kou, all will be
running smoothly once again.

Yin Kou, Liaoning, 29 July, 1976

SHENYANG

Over a century of torture was
suffered by China's Northeast;
Foreign imperialism leeched away
land and treasure, rotten warlords
battened on the common folk, but did not
resist real enemies; rebels

111

took to the mountains and forests
in long resistance struggle; until
finally out of the furnace
rose the city of Shenyang which
foreign imperialism had held
as its own, a city which became
one of the industrial hubs for
the new China.

And now along its streets
lined with tall housing of workers
where flower-pots brighten the windows,
barelegged children play happily through
their summer holiday, and in the factories
miracles are made with machinery
that at long last now takes its proper place
in serving the people rather than
an assorted gang of moneybags.

Shenyang. Old trees in Peiling*,
children who swim alongside me in
pleasant afternoons, arms flashing,
eyes laughing, as they cut through
the water. Shenyang where the future
is being built so triumphantly.

Shenyang, Liaoning, August 6, 1976

---

*Peiling: Northern Imperial Tombs.

TANGSHAN EARTHQUAKE

Over this swirling ball of mud
we call our world, that is just
a fraction of our universe, and our
universe just one of so many
reaching out ad infinitum, there

ever come strains that twist
its surface, bringing havoc
to all that people have built on it
so painstakingly.

Such a one ripped through Haicheng
and Yin Kou in 1975; then as if
damage enough had not been done,
there came another this 1976,
continuing to test the resilience
of the people, devastating the city
of Tangshan, challenging the endurance
of all to rebuild it.

The people met the blow, buried their dead,
sent injured to hospitals in
surrounding cities, and straightway
set out to try to make an evil thing
into a good one, so that life in
the reconstructed areas would be better
than ever before. Folk who know
that if they stand together they
can master the worst; so that one
knows well the fifteen thousand miners,
the fourteen thousand potters, iron and
steel, cement and fertiliser workers
are already thinking of how soon
they can carry their production forward
once more, coal from the mines filling
ships at Chinhuangtao, porcelain from
the fingers of potters going around
the wide world, showing in its loveliness;
some of the great spirit that created
the old Tangshan and will most certainly
create the new.

Shenyang, Liaoning, August 9, 1976

113

OIL PORT

The men of the first Emperor
of Chin brought the Great Wall
down to the shores of Pohai Bay
and there they built a tower high
calling it one for "viewing the sea",
and south of it there remained the name
of the Island of the King of Chin,
"Chinhuangtao", a couple of millennia later
To become a peninsula and
a coal harbour for the imperialist-seized
Kailan Mines.

Today the old harbour grows, and a new
coal harbour is under construction,
while daringly out into the bay there runs
a wall to make the new harbour
where tankers come in to load oil
that has come down 1152 kilometres from
the Taching oilfields by a new pipeline.

All that remains
of the old tower and the end
of the Great Wall, is some rubble, and
a memory; but here in this pipeline
as daringly conceived was a new Great Wall.
Black gold flows out on it to tankers and continues
by branch pipeline all the way
down to Peking refineries, 355 kilometres more
south west. The China which, the old order said,
had no oil at all, is now rich enough
to build new oil ports, carry oil on
to its great urban centres; oil for
the energy needed to lift old
burdens, and to change livelihood; oil
for air fleets, sea fleets and for the new
mechanisation that will make old
farm lands produce ever more richly.

Chinhuangtao, Hopei, 10 August, 1976

114

FUSHUN

What vast wealth comes from
the workers' hands in Fushun!
So many of the basics that
the people need to lift them
clear of poverty and chaos
into the society they plan.

All around us is busy industry
until we go up a valley, and see
a dam and a reservoir on whose
waters into the evening we reach
mountain valleys, now become
lake; great white clouds are
reflected, forests march
down to the water's edge.

So much beauty, yet bitter in one's thought
the evidence we had seen that very
morning, of the massacre at
Ping Ting Shan, where a village was surrounded
by Japanese gendarmes, homes
burned, while the people mustered under
a cliff were ruthlessly slain,
a whole three thousand of them,
and finally buried under earth
flung from the cliff top. And now, in these days,
earth has been removed from one section,
leaving a mass of bones, skulls, exposed;
a tangled mass of remains, so that walking
the eighty metres to see them all, seemed
a never-ending trail of horror. A clear thing new
generations can see and learn from,
a classroom exhibit from real life of
the rottenness of imperialism,
can we say, as dazed with the
beastliness of it all we came out
into the bright light of a Fushun day.

Fushun, Liaoning, 13 August, 1976

115

WE WILL OVERCOME

With memories of Haicheng
and Yin Kou still fresh in the
minds of all in North East China
came yet another great shake
as the earth moved with one
sharp shock after the other
in Tangshan and places around,
leaving its trail of dead and dying,
sick and injured, wrecked homes
and factories; then even before
the echoes had faded away, arrived
one more quake, this time where fighters of the
Long March crossed out of Apa to Kansu.

Ever have the Chinese people been
forced to suffer blows from nature
like these, along with flood,
drought, famine, insect pests,
warlord armies, feudal officials,
landlords, and then over all the
greedy fingers of foreign imperialism;
so that bred in people's bones
came the ability to take hard knocks
giving folk a stubborn determination
to fight back, try to overcome
each bitter thing, and somehow wrest
from it new victory. Victory of which they now
        become
ever more sure, as armed with new thinking
they gain well-organised strength to struggle
and overcome.

Earthquakes may still shatter
but the spirit of the people now becomes
too tough to be broken, making it certain that
out of the rubble and ashes of Tangshan

will rise a city still more splendid; for the people
will overcome.

Shenyang, Liaoning, 22 August, 1976

MEIHSIEN

Bicycles carrying
two hundred kilograms of stone;
commune folk who straighten rivers,
chop off hilltops and make
new plains, terrace steep
hillsides so that they will carry
tea oil bushes. "Our land is mostly
hills, then let us eat the hills",
they seem to say. "The soil is red
but so are our hearts!" For centuries
Hakka folk have faced one trial
after another. Now working together
with all neighbours, new problems
that come as a part of change
are easier to meet, though no
smaller in stature. Meihsien, where
people, an integral part of ancient
China, came and called their
new land, "Ke Yin Chou"; and then
later from here spread right out
into the four seas. Now on the quiet-flowing
Mei Kiang, long narrow boats
with slender prows glide under
a tall new bridge that so casually
spans the waters. New construction
rises, new machines make more
machines; and in peace linked with
struggle the people move on
stage to new stage, irrevocably.

Meihsien, Kwangtung, 9 November, 1976

117

HAINAN ONCE AGAIN

The clouds opened; below us lay
careful grain fields right up
to where surf beat on the beach;
a channel crossed, then once again
the shores of Hainan lie beneath us.
Abruptly we are in Haikou, palms swaying,
then the broad highways of this
Island of Rubber, its flowers and fruits
open in front of us. We pause in
the Botanical Gardens of Nada, think
of Su Tung-po and his years in this
Tan Chou, then, fascinated, see things
commune farmers have been able to do
in land reclamation; then go south
through ever-spreading rubber plantations
and forest into the new county
of Tunchang, a place which, when I
was born, was merely dense jungle,
but now is rolling downs, farmed
by folk amongst whom the spirit of Tachai
has taken firm root, so that together
they do miracles. People whose forefathers
left impossible conditions in old Fukien,
Kwangtung, Kwangsi, carving out tiny
grain fields, exploited, oppressed but
still struggling; while up on mountain sides
Li and Miao folk watched and wondered;
until the breath of revolution began
to move all common folk — Hainan becoming
a guerilla base against the old order —
heralding change that swept cleanly
over all the mainland, then penetrated
deep into Hainan hills and valleys,
stirring hearts and hands
to create all again.

Tunchang, Hainan Island, Kwangtung, 22 November, 1976

TUNCHANG

No longer young, yet with hand slasher
she attacks the stump of a tree,
hacking away at roots, while near her
a boy, perhaps grandson, shovels
at levelling a hillock, as though
it were the enemy; a bunch of girls
laugh as they drag a boulder from out of
the field-to-be. And all over
the downs of Tunchang, this
little scene is being re-enacted
a thousand times or more; tools
flash in the morning sunlight, and
red banners give colour to
the landscape. Here, production
and politics now move together
hand in hand. As the quality of life
is enriched, so do people
fight more toughly to make
the old wilderness into a really
new land. Electric power they
have generated runs through
high tension wires they have erected;
pumps they have made spray
irrigation over sugar plantations
they have reclaimed from barren lands;
and all around the people resurgent
look for new problems to master.

Tunchang really does copy Tachai
on the grand scale. Surely the canvas
is wider, the grasses more lush, but
the fire that moves hearts is the same.

Wind rustles through the tall
sugar cane. I think of Tunchang
in the future, and smile.
Tunchang, Hainan Island, Kwangtung, 23 November, 1976

NEVER REALISING

Sunlight glints on the leaves
of orange trees beside. A commune
schoolboy, short clothes a light brown
coloured by some forest dye, bag
of books on back, hoe over one shoulder
carrying-basket at the other end,
a broad palm leaf hat thrown back,
halts a moment or two to look across
downs lying in their afternoon warmth;
bare legs tanned by the suns of
a summer gone by, beautifully-formed
bare feet, and a big toe that etches
a design on the sandy path; then
a smile that includes the whole
wide world of folk like himself;
never realising how near the centre
of things he stands, in his quiet
casual magnificence.

Tunchang, Hainan Island, Kwangtung, 24 November, 1976

CHIUNG CHUNG

A city set amongst forested hills;
new centre of Li, Miao and Han
who fought and struggled here
stubbornly all through the dark
years, against a rotten, decadent,
viciously wicked order, with the
same kind of thinking that slaughtered
villagers in nearby Vietnam. The old
Kuomintang made no friends amongst
the peoples of Chiung Chung, simply
reducing folk to be a dying remnant.

But the people's fighters came back,
and today new life really surges
through the hills of Chiung Chung,
around the Five Finger Mountain,
by rubber plantations and ever
bigger paddy fields, through the doors
of schools, hospitals, factories, all
so newly here — changes made creating
bases for vast changes yet to come.

Chiung Chung, Hainan Island, Kwangtung, 25 November, 1976

WHERE THE DEER LOOKED BACK

There was a beauty and a dynamism
about the Li-Miao capital of Tungtze
that stayed fragrantly with us
as we swept down the broad highway
through rubber and tea plantations to
Hainan's southern coast, where lies
the place they call Lu Hwei Tou:
a gem set by the placid and blue sea —
tall palms and many a pleasant tree
surrounding, scent of tree and sea
combining.

Lu Hwei Tou — "The Deer Turns his Head" —
poetic name enough for this piece
of tropical loveliness: ocean-going ships
lie sleepily in the harbour; fishing
trawlers line the wharves by the Ngai Hsien
county seat, and west along the coast we go
to enjoy the scenery and fishermen's children
at Tien Ya Hai Chiao, where Kuo Mo-jo
has left a poem, engraved on a great boulder
rock, and harvesters of the sea bring in

121

their catch of herrings. Then back we go
to the calm serenity of Lu Hwei Tou,
realising why Anna Louise loved it so
in her declining years. Children climb
coconut palms, one boy going high
laughingly pushing down the big nuts
with his bare feet. A cadre from Ngai Hsien
tells of new records in grain production
and plans for new irrigation, power generation . .
We swim at a glorious beach, refreshed
and ready for the long road north
to a Peking winter again.

Lu Hwei Tou, Ngai Hsien, Hainan Island, Kwangtung,
29 November, 1976

FANG SHAN COUNTY IN PEKING

Fable states that the Queen Mother
of the Western Heavens, Hsi Wang Mu,
lived high up on the mountain-top
of I Fang Shan. History states that
under Peking's imperial rule, earth
from Fang Shan was brought each year
to the Altar of Agriculture in
symbolic tribute.

Then there was the Fang Shan
of modern history, where peasants
rose and fought with heroism against
first Japanese, then Kuomintang
oppression; so many gallant actions
unsung and now forgotten except
in the tales old folk tell as they
sit around over pots of tea under
a winter sun; soon they too will

be gone and old stories will fade out
into the mountain mist.

Fang Shan, where earliest man
yet found in China, left his remains,
and where now people work in factory
and commune making both produce
ever more richly, despite all difficulty.
Fang Shan, with a new town centre now
rising, fine jewel in the diadem
of Greater Peking.

Fang Shan, Peking, 11 March, 1977

ON THINGS AS THEY ARE

If you own anything really
valuable, there will be gangs
who would like to steal. If
your land is rich in people,
there will be those who
exploit your folk for cheap
labour, and flood the world with
the goods they turn out.
Thieving monopoly will ever
support your establishment with
rake-offs of one kind or another.
If you fall for feudalistic forms
the rascals will brightly embellish
these, modernising them for
your happy consumption; if you live
for fun and games, why, fun and games
will be made a priority, to the exclusion
of most else. There is nothing
the enemy will stick at doing, nowhere
he will not infiltrate. Even China,

with all its vast strength, had its gang
of four and their minions to sap
and subvert. The land of the October
revolution is not the land Lenin
would have had, even though his picture
is on so many walls. Often there are
more enemies within than without, those
who breed cynicism, hopelessness,
cunningly splitting, putting lush
comfort first in living, always
intriguing for power at any price.
Insatiable greed, and the lust for
control are universal weaknesses.
To love and serve the people, the opposite
concept; and on whether the weakness of the one
or the basic strength of the other wins out, depends
the future of our world of peoples.

Tsinan, Shantung, 17 March, 1977

OLD BASE — NEW COUNTRYSIDE

Once hills and downs around Chu Nan
formed a strong revolutionary base
for wars of resistance
and liberation; over a thousand
people's fighters died here —
so that on a hilltop near
the county centre, a slender pagoda
rises above the pines like a sharp
exclamation mark, in memory of them.

No ordinary hilltop, this, but one
where the enemy had emplaced a gun
which was promptly seized by the people's
guerilla fighters, and used against him.

The people of Chu Nan are still good
fighters, winning many an action
through the long years since
vanguard brigades of what is now
a Tachai county make bad lands
into good lands, a tumbled mass
of mountain ravines and eroded
downs into irrigated fields
that stand up against drought,
rip stone slabs from mountain
sides to build new housing,
aqueducts, irrigation works; make
many sacrifices for the benefit
of all, showing that the spirit
that brought down the old, can
really create the new.

Chu Nan, Shantung, 23 March, 1977

LINKS

One remembers well times
when, if natural disaster
struck, the area was
closed off, the people left
to work things out as best
they could; even if there
were a railway as in Inner Mongolia
in the late twenties, the starving
had no money to buy grain brought
in; they simply died by the wayside.

Now all China becomes linked with
a common idea and her highways, railways,
canals strong links in the chain
that holds all together, each part

of the system depending on the other
so that with a disaster on the scale
of the Tangshan, earthquake relief
streams in from every quarter.

Never a good thing, but that
a bad one shows its ugly head.
The gang of four had enough power
to pitch wrenches into the machine;
out to wreck and bring chaos, not only
in Tangshan but all over the land,
playing with the lives and hopes
of the multi-millions.

How then can they be forgiven?
How looked upon without disgust
by all who felt their trust
arrogantly, flippantly betrayed!
How great a lesson is this
to be learned by students of
revolution whose aim is to link
the working folk of all lands
even more securely together.

Chu Nan, Shantung, 23 March, 1977

SEEN IN CHU NAN

Climbing round a rocky mountainside
a whole row of cherry trees in full
blossom greets us cheerfully, the scene
suddenly changed to one of serene
loveliness, with grey stones
as background only.

At the Willow Tree Valley of
the Kuo family, we listen to tales

126

of the times of total illiteracy,
and how change came in; and there too
out of the stone of the mountainside
a new assembly hall is built, where
youth stages a concert, bright and vivid.

Then there is the Pang Tuan Brigade
that follows the lead of its research
station in digging deeper
into cause and effect in land work,
organising its folk around science
so that it becomes a centre for
better seeds, better method, better
livelihood to all, for the revolution
to build its base upon.

Chu Nan, where all
are geared to the struggle
for livelihood, right down
to the children who collect
saltpetre from the base
of old walls, to help in the making of
explosives.

Good to have come to Chu Nan,
live awhile, catch something
of its spirit; for before one sets
out to teach, it is best to try and learn.

Chu Nan, South Shantung, 24 March, 1977

H S I P O

Shanghai of the thirties, and
the thoughtful face of the
big-framed Hans Shippe looked

quizzically at me, as he wondered
if I had caught the significance
of a formulation he had made.

Now today I stand in front
of a massive tomb of Hsi Po, as
this German friend became known,
in a quiet memorial park in
Lin Yi, South Shantung, and hear
some of the story of his passing,
that cold autumn morning now
well over three decades ago.

The internationalism of the working
people of the world is still
a tender shoot, yet the Chinese
Revolution has attracted some
who have been willing to die for it
knowing of its promise for all people;
and of these is Hsi Po
whose name lives on around the old
fighting area of Yi Meng Shan.

The bullets of imperialism thudded
into his body, making it lifeless,
a part of the good earth again; but
the spirit that moved him goes on
moving others in many quarters
of our world where more and more folk
come together in struggle for
the better way.

Lin Yi, South Shantung, 25 March, 1977

T A I   S H A N

A commune brigade wall made up
of rubble, and from it a fragment

of ancient brick looks at me,
with excised pattern of the sun
rising out of the sea, making
me wonder how many the sight seen
at dawn from Tai Shan's summit
has moved. All those emperors
and their courts down through
two millennia of history, who have
come in procession to this Eastern Peak
and worshipped here, as did their ancestors
long before them in the dim light
of pre-history.

In the Tai Miao that lies below
the foot of the ascent
an eighty-year-old gardener
reaches sure hands amongst greenhouse flowers,
    preparing
to move them out as days warm up;
straight, erect, he takes my hand
in firm grip and I feel that here so surely
is the unquenchable spirit of Tai Shan.

A few decades past, the mountain top
looked out over decaying temples,
wide, stony river beds, barren hillsides,
and a landlord-ridden countryside; today
it sees factories and schools along
its lower slopes, reservoirs, orchards
in blossom, green cypresses
reaching ever higher, while over
the plains all has changed.
Once, in many parts of China,
a stone would be erected, carved
deep with the characters
"Tai Shan Stone! Don't Dare!"
as warning against evil spirits.
Today the whole of Tai Shan's

message as it stands so serenely
is "Dare and Dare Again!"

Tai An, Shantung, 25 March, 1977

WRITTEN IN KAN LO, DA LIANG SHAN

Laugh with the sun
and the freshening breeze
laugh with the leaves
dancing on trees, laugh
for the people they call
the Yis, who now have come
down from hilltops to valleys
and set about to change
all again; folk out of a slave
society reaching for socialism;
jolted out of the past, first
by the Long March, then by
the Liberation Army which later
brought in engineers to build
the railway that has tied all
to the rest of China, bringing
new horizons, new challenge
so that Tachai is not just
a name, but a place farmers
can go to see, become fired
with the will to emulate.

No longer is it Han against Yi,
nor Black Yi against White Yi,
Lord against a crouching slave;
now it is Yi and Han together
building a new society amongst
the mass of mountains they call

the Liang Shan; bringing in
new ways, new hope to the poor
and hopeless of a bitter past;
for those who were asleep have
awakened, and looking at their
own strong hands, smile.

Kan Lo, Da Liang Shan, Szechuan, 12 April, 1977

A MOUNTAIN TOWN CELEBRATES

Tall mountains standing like
sentinels around, cloaked in
light blue haze, and down the street
of the valley town of Kan Lo
marches a procession of ten thousand
children of schools, commune folk,
workers, medical cadres, a mass
of colour and movement led by
the revolutionary committee with
Chu Lin in the centre; Chu Lin,
once the frequently beaten, often
re-sold slave boy who now
leads the poor and oppressed who
today are lords of the land
they make give them new livelihood.

Proudly those who suffered
under the old society can march
today with bitter memories relegated
to the past, and but the future
to work out in line with the teachings
of the old leader, the new volume
of whose works all welcome so cheerfully
this bright Da Liang Shan day.

Kanlo, Szechuan, 15 April, 1977

131

O MEI SHAN

How many poems have been written
on the glories of O Mei Shan, how
many tears have fallen, how much
blood has flowed over the land
below it in old struggles;
then, too, how many, a countless
many, have felt uplifted and
refreshed after climbing the heights
and immersing themselves in
the beauties of this gem of
scenic glory. Now I sit at its feet
looking down through forest trees
at a valley reservoir below,
glad of the chance to absorb some
of the serenity around, pondering over
the so few thousand years in which
peoples have made such gigantic strides;
wondering whether the human mind
can keep up with the breathless
rate of technical advance, while
staying in tune with environment,
ever reaching out to other folk
who work, to gain common understanding.

Once on O Mei were over a hundred temples,
now there are around twenty-five;
but on the foothills of the mountain
a great university stands,
with eager students going out to work
on the highways of their land.

Yes, O Mei Shan is like
a giant exclamation mark; running
straight down the precipice from
its summit, in all its loveliness,
demanding that peoples think, and
think again, guide hands so that

there will be the leisure to make
more parks like this one, where
one and all can come and many feel
that one of the ways to better
understanding may lie up ridges, along
mountain tracks, and through quiet
forests, where minds can rest
and prepare for action again.

O Mei Shan, Szechuan, 20 April, 1977

MEI SHAN HOME OF SU TUNG-PO

Strange how a poet of almost
a millennium past should have
with the strength and beauty
of his verse remained in the
minds of his people, his works
annotated, collected, cut on
stone tablets, all surviving
to this day, part of the
traditional culture of a people,
sure of their respect.

The characters he wrote
are each a model of artistry
but I look at the children
playing around pavilions
and courtyards, wondering
if in their lives they have
to achieve so great a perfection
in just methodology to express
themselves, and know that either
these or their descendants will
one day as the common language
spreads, change to a script that
any child can learn easily, not
as an end in itself, but as a tool

for swifter learning, leaving
the grand old characters to savants
to specialise in and admire.

Truly this old home of Su Tung-po
is a stately, colourful memorial
that through long years to come
people from many quarters
will want to visit and catch
some of its quiet charm
and the sense of history it leaves.

Mei Shan, Szechuan, 22 April, 1977

STRAY THOUGHTS ON LIN YUIN SHAN

The giant Buddha of Lin Yuin Shan
at today's Lo Shan, looks out from
the red rock from which he is carved,
seventy-one metres high, serenely
over the confluence of three great rivers
as he has done for the past twelve
or more centuries, calmly waiting.
The afternoon sun lights up his figure,
evening mists put a gossamer blanket
around his feet, early summer leaves
sweep over his head. A bold conception
by some bygone artist, which he has
left succeeding generations; and looking
at his face one wonders just what
he is trying to say. Maybe that people
can only gain understanding by struggling
for it; all are learners; teachers
cannot do more than give method, tell of
experience, both positive and negative.

That it matters not whether a person
is naked or prettily tailored, ragged
or bemedalled, it is his thinking
that matters; has he developed character
or does he just live to grab? Can
he live and work with other workers
regardless of race or colour, or is
he content to be tied down to an exploiting
class? Does he live by values
insidiously indoctrinated by that
society, which can have but one ending?
Are peoples to inherit the earth
and all therein, or are they to go on
as did petty chieftains of primitive
days? Soon any country can use
fast breeding to produce enough
plutonium to disintegrate the world.

Just stray thoughts on a Lo Shan evening,
looking across the rivers at the image
that seems to ponder so deeply. A fresh
breeze springs up, sails fill, boats
glide past; and a friend comes to tell
of what can be done when people
work in harmony together.

Lo Shan, Szechuan, 17 April, 1977

MEI SHAN MEMORIES

Su Tung-po, of the time of Sung,
practical administrator, great poet,
whose old home is now a park
and museum, keeps Mei Shan in touch
with the past; school children who
join with the masses of fighters
against the depredations of a sprawling

135

Min River, are a bright omen for
its future, showing how the old
revolutionary ideas of practical
service, regardless of self, still have
strong hold. Commune members
have made Mei Hsien a model for
this present, encouraging other counties
to follow its lead as it follows Tachai.

Mei Hsien where the wrong policies
of the gang of four can now be looked on
as just accidents of history, to be
studied, learned from . . At the Kwang Hua
Commune on Min River banks, grandmothers,
and then mothers with babies strapped
to their backs, together pluck baskets of
rose petals from the mass of bushes
that liven up early summer here, and all
around the air is full of perfume . .
Sweet are the memories that linger, when
one thinks back on Mei Shan.

Chiang Lai, Szechuan, 24 April, 1977

HEI HO EVENING

Smoke rises from many chimneyed
houses; outside our compound
an electrician walks up a pole
to fix a lamp; two small fry stop
trying to crawl under iron gates
to watch in admiration. Long summer
evenings make them a time for kids
to play and elders to walk, meet
friends, and discuss.

We rest and think back on visits

made here; the Huang Chi Ying Brigade
where descendants of old-time Manchu
Bannermen now farm so successfully
as part of the vanguard Aihwei Commune.
Here on the right bank is a sandspit
island, practically part of brigade land
but claimed by Imperialist Russia, who
reasons that having stolen the other bank
everything in the river is theirs, for
have they not built a propaganda city
on old Hai Lan Bao to show how big
and mighty they are in contrast to the simple
commune homes the new rich despise?
Sunset changes the dark river
into a glittering crimson, good
omen for bright dawns yet to come.

At night we go to a concert
in the people's theatre of Hei Ho,
where pretty Aihwei children dance
and a Shanghai singer captivates
with her song; she one of many
who have come to these border regions,
serving brilliantly.

Hei Ho, Heilungkiang, 11 June, 1977

OLUNCHUN VILLAGE

Deep in forested hills
clear streams run through groves of
silver birch; lilies of the valley
with a glory of other wild flowers
on my table; children around
with the light of dawn in their eyes;
in the big school playground
they swing high around a pole

137

on ropes; youngsters who today
look at the few simple utensils
and tents erected teepee fashion
by the riverside, in display, as curios almost;
Now folk herd more deer than
they shoot, use mechanisation to
plow, cultivate, sow and reap, so
that their village attains more
material comforts for its working folk
than many a city has, representing
a successful integration of old and new,
minority and Han, city folk and
those of the forests, Shanghai dialect
mixing with the hill air, the good
points of all making this highland
valley a place of increasing beauty.
How then could one not love
the new Olunchun?

Hsing Seng Commune, Aihwei, Heilungkiang,
11 June, 1977

THE EPIC OF TACHING

Fleecy clouds high in a dazzling sky
over the vast plains around Taching;
Taching, a name now with magic to it,
for by the gallantry and sacrifice
of workers there it becomes a model
for industry the whole land over.
How many secrets has mother nature held
until that of how to use the strength
of the working people was found
and activated. All through the dark
years, a great sea of black gold lay
in waiting, while armies of invaders

trampled madly over the surface of
Northeastern provinces, looting, burning,
thinking to grab all for themselves,
forcing the people to build railways
for them, so that they might further
exploit. And over the plains
around the marshes of Taching, then
known simply as "Saertu", shepherds tended
flocks in summer, and winds howled
over snowy wastes in winter.

Now on a summer's day, all seems
so quiet; white installations
set amongst greenery, silent until
one puts an ear against pipes
and hears the flowing sound of oil
that will run through pipelines
to coastal ports, and too to Peking,
making millions grateful to the workers
of Taching who have given so much
to make the black gold flow.

Taching, Heilungkiang, 5 June, 1977

A NOTE ON TWO FAMOUS DOCTORS

Dr George Hatem (Dr Ma Hai-teh) an American of Lebanese extraction, came to China as a young doctor in 1933, following medical studies in the U.S.A., Beirut and Switzerland. Dr Hans Miller also came to China from Switzerland six years later. Each responded early to the need of the Red Army for doctors and each identified himself with the Chinese Revolution in devoted service to the Chinese people. They are now naturalised Chinese. Following liberation Dr Ma Hai-teh's outstanding achievement has been his part in China's eradication of syphilis; while Dr Miller's lifework has been crowned with success in the movement to put an end to opium addiction. (Read *China: The Quality of Life*, Wilfred Burchett with Rewi Alley, Penguin Books, 1976, for further information and references.)

NOTES by Rewi Alley on the Chinese provinces and places he has travelled while writing some of these poems.

Hainan Island

This is a part of Kwangtung Province, lying off its south coast. Its climate is largely tropical, there being many plantations of rubber, tea, coffee and other products. The south part of the island is the Li-Miao Autonomous Chou, the Li and Miao being hill people of that region. It has a population of over five million people.

Heilungkiang

The huge Northeastern province which borders on the USSR. It has, in its southern basin, one of the world's big oil-fields, that of Taching, which today is a model for all Chinese industry. It has over 30,000,000 people scattered over its vast area.

Kwangtung

The southern province of which Kwangchow — once called Canton — is the capital.

Meihsien is a prefecture of a number of counties in the East River area of Kwangtung. It is the home of the Hakka people, who came down from the North in historic times. They once called their home Ke Yin-chou. Many Hakka people now live overseas, and also in different parts of Kwangtung and Kwangsi Provinces.

Swatow Prefecture lies along the Southeast coast of Kwangtung, the city of that name replacing the ancient trading and porcelain-producing port of Chaochow on the mouth of the now silted-up Han River. Swatow has a big population for a limited amount of land, so that industry is increasingly developed.

Liaoning

The Northeastern province once called South Manchuria by the Japanese who occupied it from 1931 onwards.

Peitaiho, Chinhuangtao

In the Tangshan Prefecture, Northeast Hopei.

Shansi

The highland province, west of Peking.

Shantung

China's second largest province, with 70,000,000 people in it. Once scourged with wars, drought, floods and famine, it now stands up on its own, and makes an old land a new one.

Sinkiang

This is a frontier province in China's far Northwest bordering on India, Pakistan, Afghanistan, the Soviet Union and Mongolia. The area is five times the size of France. It has over eleven million people divided into many nationalities, and is called the Sinkiang Uigher Autonomous Region.

Szechuan

The huge province in Southwest China, in which is the rich plain, the Red Basin. It has 90,000,000 people. Its minorities are Tibetan, Yi and Miao, who live amongst its mountains.